"Take it from someone who knows, it's ne[...]
season of unspeakable pain. I wish during my own dark seasons I [...]
had this life-giving book. I'm grateful for this valuable resource to point
others to. There is light ahead, and Josh will help you experience it."

—**Gene Appel,** Senior Pastor, Eastside Christian Church, Anaheim, CA

"Our lives forever changed when I came out of the darkness of drug
addiction into the light of Jesus Christ. Recovery is a major theme
throughout *Re\entry*. If you are in darkness, there is hope to find purpose
in your life. If you are a believer in Jesus Christ, you are in recovery.
But maybe your mission has become cloudy. You won't leave unchanged
reading *Re\entry*. You will see how entry and reentry draws us into the
heart of God and into more meaningful lives."

—**Mac Owen,** Celebrate Recovery National Director; and
Mary Owen, Celebrate Recovery National Training Coach Director

"From one of the coldest and darkest places on earth, Josh Ross enlightens
readers with incredible insight. *Re\entry* is a wonderful guide through
the dark times, thirsty droughts, and cold spells of our lives and helps
us find the peace that comes from the true Light of the world. Get this
book and reap its blessings for your life!"

—**Al Robertson,** from A&E's *Duck Dynasty*, author, *A New Season*

"We want a guide who's faced the fears of darkness and lived to tell about it.
I've learned through the years that we can't fully appreciate the brightness
and beauty of the light without experiencing the darkness. I highly
recommend this book from Josh because he's qualified experientially
and biblically to be your guide to the light."

—**Chris Conlee,** Senior Pastor, High Point Church, author, *Love Works*

"Any pastoral book worth its salt comes from the crucible of experience
and suffering. Josh tells a great story with a pastoral heart for others who
are searching for their way out of the darkness."

—**Drew and Ellie Holcomb,** recording artists

"In *Re\entry*, Josh Ross leverages his own life experiences to help us see
God's grace as the focal point of life. When our world crashes and despair
attempts to steal the little hope we have left, it's refreshing to know that
God's grace means we're never hopeless."

—**Caleb Kaltenbach,** Lead Pastor, Discovery Church, author,
Messy Grace and *God of Tomorrow*

"By the time you turn the last page of this book, you will feel like you've shared an incredible conversation over a wonderful meal with the author. More importantly, you'll leave the table knowing you're not alone, because everyone who takes a seat at God's table is after the same thing—healing. Our world is fluent in suffering, and Josh does an incredible job of helping us understand its purpose. You won't regret reading this book."

—**Jon Weece,** Senior Pastor, Southland Christian Church, Lexington, Kentucky

"We all desire to walk in light, but we don't always know how to make the readjustments. Josh Ross does an amazing job showing us how to walk in the light. This book raises the light of God's gracious truth at a level that is restorative and enlightening."

—**Dr. Stacy Spencer,** Senior Pastor, New Directions Christian Church, Memphis

"He's not a travel agent telling you about places he's never been before. Josh is no stranger to pain, and he embodies the sacred rhythms of which he writes. Re\entry is refreshingly candid, biblically faithful, and preeminently helpful for anyone looking to sustain a new beginning in their lives."

—**Chris Seidman,** Lead Minister, The Branch Church, author, *Heaven on Earth*

"A wonderful exploration of God's relentless invitation to pursue a life of hope, adventure, and joy. I highly recommend it."

—**Ian Morgan Cron,** author of bestselling book *Jesus, My Father, the CIA and Me* and *The Road Back to You*

"Ross's personable account draws the reader in and asks us to consider what it truly means to move from darkness into light. We all share that journey, and Josh gives us the language and understanding we need to embrace it within ourselves and appreciate it in others."

—**Suzanne Stabile,** cofounder and Animator of Life in the Trinity Ministry, coauthor, *The Road Back to You*

"While some adventures are exciting and beautiful, life can also take us on expeditions through darkness, pain, and isolation that we neither desire nor are prepared for. Having lived through his own seasons of darkness, Josh Ross gives us a path and plan to come home to God after life's twists take us on excursions we wouldn't necessarily choose."

—**Sean Palmer,** Teaching Pastor, Ecclesia Houston, author, *Unarmed Empire*; and **Chris Seay,** Lead Pastor, Ecclesia Houston, author, *A Place at the Table*

RE\ENTRY

RE\ENTRY

How pain, roots, and rhythm guide us

from darkness to light

JOSH ROSS

LEAFWOOD
PUBLISHERS
an imprint of Abilene Christian University Press

RE\ENTRY

How Pain, Roots, and Rhythm Guide Us from Darkness to Light

LEAFWOOD
PUBLISHERS
an imprint of Abilene Christian University Press

Copyright © 2017 by Josh Ross

ISBN 978-0-89112-485-6

Printed in the United States of America

Book published in association with Ambassador Literary Agency, P.O. Box 50358, Nashville, TN 37205.

Library of Congress Cataloguing in Publication Data is on file at the Library of Congress, Washington, DC.

Cover design by ThinkPen Design, LLC
Interior text design by Sandy Armstrong, Strong Design

Leafwood Publishers is an imprint of Abilene Christian University Press
ACU Box 29138
Abilene, Texas 79699

1-877-816-4455
www.leafwoodpublishers.com

17 18 19 20 21 22 / 7 6 5 4 3 2 1

To my wife, Kayci.

*When I think of the forms of darkness (pain, unhealthy
anger, brokenness, grief, and loneliness) God has walked me
through in my life as an adult, you are right there next to
Jesus as one who constantly points me to his light.*

You are a gift to me.

I love you.

Contents

Acknowledgments

The town of Barrow welcomed me as if I had been part of their community for years. A special thanks to the management of the Airport Inn. Not only did you provide me with a clean, warm room, but you helped me navigate my way through a town I knew little about. Thank you, Pastor Matthews, Pastor Sciaro, and former Barrow High School principal Bev Gillaspie for carving out time for me. You extended hospitality to a complete stranger. Thank you.

This trip to Barrow would not have happened without financial support. To Ben and Stephanie Smith, Randy and Brenda Frederick, Mark and Stephanie Taylor, Glenn and Marie Hailey, Tom and Jeannie Alexander, and Rick and Beverly Ross, thank you for believing in me, and in this project.

Kyle Taylor, thank you for joining me on this adventure. Neither of us knew what we were getting into, but I am grateful I didn't walk this journey alone. You are a good friend, and a creative genius.

Ralph Bryant, when I willingly walked through a season of intentional sin back in 1997, God used you to speak truth and grace into my heart. I didn't know it at the time, but God used you to teach me about the power of *reentry into the light*. Thank you for taking a few extra minutes after class one day at church camp to speak redemption over me.

Mac and Mary Owen, you have lived the message of this book for years. Through you and Celebrate Recovery, the message of reentry and recovery extends to tens of thousands of people every year. You are a gift to me.

Wes Yoder, my agent and friend. You pushed me hard on this project. I just wanted to write about what I had learned from reading about Barrow. You told me I had to go. I'm glad I listened. I appreciate you more than you know.

Leafwood Publishing, thank you Jason Fikes, Mary Hardegree, Duane Anderson, and the entire Leafwood team. You weren't afraid to push me, challenge me, and encourage me to tweak ideas, delete what wasn't working, create new chapters, and to develop a smoother flow. Together, you helped develop something we are proud of. I couldn't have done this without you.

Memphis, for nearly a decade I have called you home. I love raising my family in this city. I love raising my family in this city. One of the greatest honors I have in Memphis is being a board member at Agape Child and Family Services. You are a kingdom effort that has taught me more about the power of reentry than I could ever fathom. I'm also grateful for the partnership with HopeWorks, Streets Ministries, Memphis Teacher Residency, Harding School of Theology, SOMA, Harding Academy, The Boys and Girls Club of Memphis, Memphis Athletic Ministries, Service Over Self, Binghampton Development Corporation, The Micah Project, Caritas Village, Choose901, and so many others who redemptively invest in our city. Memphis wouldn't be the same without you.

Sycamore View, I can't believe I get to call this my job. Being your preacher, and having you as my church family, is one of the greatest joys in my life. You have taught me so much about the message of *reentry*. Let's keep believing that God's restoration is for the 901, and for the entire world.

Rick and Beverly Ross, so much of what I believe and know about God's heart has come from you. Thank you for giving me healthy roots and rhythm.

Truitt and Noah, your mom and I want to teach you to have deep roots, yet we also know that times will come when you're going to need to hear Jesus's voice inviting you back into adventurous life again. Jesus is for you.

Kayci, you embody beauty, creativity, courage, and loyalty. You are a force in the kingdom of God. I don't want to live life or do ministry without you. Thank you for believing in me.

Foreword

by Randy Frazee

Re\entry is a book for everyone. I'm serious. You may not think that now—but trust me, your day will come. It is just the way life rolls. I had to engage in a reentry dance at the loss of my mother as Josh did with the loss of his sister. Today it might be labeled PTSD—post-traumatic stress disorder. A few days on the other side of a tragedy, when things get all quiet again, you realize something has shifted forever, externally and internally. Externally, someone is missing in your life or something has been taken away from you or you are now the owner of an illness you never dreamed would come your way. Maybe you made a very big mistake and wish you could have a redo, but in this case, it is simply not available to you. This error and the subsequent loss it brings will forever be a part of your story. Internally, there is a weariness, an anxiety, a depression that won't go away. You would run from it if you knew the source. It follows you all day long and particularly talks to you at night. Life will never be the same, or so you think. Finding the motivation to press on is virtually gone. Humiliation abounds. You know you shouldn't isolate yourself, but pretending in crowds is just too painful. So, you find yourself going it alone. This is following a big mistake with an even bigger one. If you have been here, it is not hard to know why some people think suicide would be a grand relief. Imagining life groaning on for another ten, twenty, or thirty years like this is unbearable.

So, is that it? NO, IT IS NOT! Let Josh take you on a most unusual journey to a most unusual place to lay out the road map to your reentry. From darkness into light. This is not a book that points its bony index finger in your face and tells you to "pull yourself up by your bootstraps" and get over it. Move on. It is a tender book with hope-filled steps that guides you back into a real life that can be even better than before—no joke. Reentry will require establishing two important things: roots and rhythm. Josh will effectively walk you through this as a good trail guide. Trust him. He has walked this path before and knows the way back.

Josh extended this invitation to me to write a little something about his new work. What an honor. Little did I know that another serious shift would occur in my life from the time I received the manuscript to the time I had a chance to read it. It has helped me tremendously. Now, I am not quite sure if the primary purpose of Josh's invitation was to encourage you the reader or to encourage me, a guy who needed a good reentry strategy. Maybe, just maybe, it is for both of us. The best recommendation comes from one who has been genuinely helped by a product or service. Well, I have been greatly ministered to by this book, and now I offer it up to you as you navigate your own reentry flight plan or as you come alongside a good friend who needs one.

See you on the other side!

Randy Frazee is a pastor and author of *What Happens After You Die* and *Real Simplicity: Making Room for Life* (coauthored with his wife, Rozanne).

The Gift That Gave a Girl Her Life Back

I sat in a warm room in Barrow, Alaska, looking out a window into piles of snow and built-up ice. The wind chill was minus forty. Every item of clothing on my body I had borrowed from friends.

I grew up in Dallas and now live in Memphis, so I don't own a heavy coat, hiking boots, or clothes that insulate me from the cold. In the places where I have lived, an inch of snow will shut down a city for three days. At the time, I was thirty-three years old, and I had never experienced temperatures below zero. Never.

After ringing in the New Year in Memphis, the next eight days would take me to two extremes. On the first Sunday of the New Year, my family boarded a plane to Orlando, where we played at Disney World before heading to Daytona, where I would speak at the National Conference of Youth Ministers (NCYM). The next Sunday, I boarded a plane for Barrow, Alaska. It's the northernmost city in the United States, a town I didn't even know existed a few months earlier.

On the first Monday of 2014, I walked through Disney World in a warm eighty-four degrees. The second Monday of the year, as

I walked off the plane in Barrow, I was greeted by a high temperature of twenty-seven degrees below zero, with a wind chill of forty-six below.

I had made this trip to meet the people of Barrow because I had a strong notion that this community has a lot to teach Christ-followers—and the world, for that matter—about light, darkness, surviving difficult times, and so much more.

One day, I was preparing to interview a teacher about life on the northern slope, and we were hoping her daughter, though shy, would be willing to sit down in a chair so I could ask her a few questions. I had heard her story a few days before, and the moment I took in a piece of her testimony, I knew I wanted to meet her.

You see, a few years back, when she was in the fourth grade, she fell into a deep depression. There was some stress in her life due to circumstances and relational pain, and it didn't help that it was also the season of polar night, when the sun sets in mid-November and isn't seen again until mid- to late January.

Then one day, she picked up a pencil and began to draw. The next day, she did it again. The day after that, she returned to that same place. Day after day, art became her therapy. It was the one thing that gave hope and meaning to her life. In some ways, it lifted her out of a dark season, both literally and metaphorically.

I can't help but wonder if art was a grace-gift from God to give her meaning during the darkness brought on by depression and relational dysfunction. Or was this a gift that God had given her earlier in life, but which could only be discovered and cultivated in a season of darkness?

Why Barrow?

I had traveled to Barrow because I was convinced that it had something to teach me about the rhythms of darkness and light in our world. Every human experiences these seasons of change, and the darkness drapes not simply our souls but even our communities.

This isn't a book about the culture of Barrow. It's a book about what it means to be human. It's a book about thriving with God. It's a book about reengaging the heart and mission of God when we know circumstances have changed, and life moving forward is not going to be like it was in the past.

When my sister, Jenny, tragically died in 2010, I had to find myself again. I didn't need to get saved again. Yet I knew that how I would walk with God in the future would not be the same way I had walked with him in the past. God's character and nature hadn't changed. But my experiences in life had. I had to learn to trust, surrender, and refuse to coast through life as if this life doesn't matter.

I have learned that the journey from pain to healing, from wounds to scars, and from darkness into light can often be one of the most difficult, challenging roads we are invited to walk. Maybe that is why the Bible talks so much about perseverance through all circumstances.

I have lived this through seasons of my own sin, Jenny's death, stress in ministry, betrayal, unhealthy emotions, and other tragedies.

Memphis, the city we have called home since 2008, has taught us that the journey from forms of darkness into light isn't for individuals alone; it's the march of humanity as we press forward into a brighter tomorrow.

We have all been inducted into clubs we never signed up for: widowhood, divorce, adultery, loss of a child, cancer, car wreck, bankruptcy, abuse, and neglect. The challenge is that we can choose to settle or we can press into the good news of Jesus, the One who has an amazing track record of bringing things to life . . . or back to life.

This book is for anyone who has struggled to find their way again.

This book is for those who have been held hostage by the past.

This book is for all who want to be proactive in preparing themselves now for difficult paths that will greet them in the future.

You may sit to read this book, but ultimately I hope you will join in walking as we live out this life.

CHAPTER 1

Eleven Days above the Arctic Circle

I had a few "what in the world were you thinking" moments. After preaching in Memphis at Sycamore View on the second Sunday in January, I boarded a plane for Alaska. My research into the town of Barrow showed that it was void of fast-food restaurants and recognizable franchises. I had packed dozens of peanut butter crackers and protein bars. I knew I wasn't going to an underdeveloped nation, but that didn't keep me from packing like it.

Before walking onto my connecting flight in Minneapolis, I stopped by Burger King. I ordered the biggest value meal on their menu, and I savored every bite as if there was a chance I would never eat again. Extra meat. Extra bacon. Extra jalapeños.

Upon arriving in Anchorage around 9:00 P.M., I had my first major decision to make. My flight to Barrow would leave the next morning at 6:00 A.M., so should I sleep in the airport, or pay for a hotel, knowing I would only be in the room for six hours? I've slept in airports on a number of occasions, but this time I opted for the hotel room. The thought of a hot shower and *SportsCenter* was too appealing. I couldn't resist.

I don't know much about people from Alaska. I had heard they are nice folks. I had a friend at Abilene Christian University who was from there, and he was kind, social, and seemed to be normal. Other than him, my experiences with Alaskans had basically been from documentaries and that infamous conversation Barbara Walters had with Sarah Palin.

The first person I met was a cab driver, and let's just say he woke up on the wrong side of the bed. His attitude was as if Beyoncé's sister, Solange, had just roughed him up in an elevator. He wasn't into conversation, and I finally gave up trying after he made it known that his vocabulary consisted of about seven words, all consisting of four letters.

The next morning, I walked into the Anchorage airport knowing that the next time I stepped off a plane I would be in Barrow. I had been anticipating this trip for over six months. I was eager to learn, but my anxiety about being in the frigid cold easily outweighed my eagerness to understand the values and principles that carry the people of that community through harsh winters.

I tapped the weather app on my phone one more time. It read −24°F. I should have closed the app, but I didn't. I hit the button that revealed the wind-chill factor: −41°F. In my mind, I began to say good-bye to Kayci and the boys, as if I wasn't sure I was going to make it. I'm from Texas. I hate the cold.

I was raised in Dallas, went to school in Abilene, and then moved to Houston before relocating to Memphis. There were days living in Abilene when I thought I was going to freeze to death. I remember walking to class with the weather in the low twenties. To make it worse, the wind would blow around thirty miles per hour. I would walk fast, bury my face in my coat, and pray for Jesus to come back.

Abilene is a city in West Texas. Some people have described that part of the state as the section that is so flat you can watch your dog run away for about ten days. There are no mountains, hills, or even trees to stop the wind. But the coldest days I experienced in Abilene were still forty degrees warmer than where I was about to land in Barrow.

I boarded the flight saying to myself, "Seriously, what were you thinking?"

Adventures May Take Us Miles from Home

So, what drew me to the northernmost town—the northernmost point—in the United States?

In the spring of 2013, while researching material for a sermon I was preparing to preach on Jesus being the light of the world, I came across a 2005 article in the *New York Times* that mentioned Barrow.[1] I was interested in the impact that a lengthy season of darkness may have on an individual and a community. What I discovered in that short article took hold of my imagination, and it would send me over 3,400 miles away from home, and over 330 miles above the Arctic Circle.

Barrow is the northernmost city in the United States, and it is home to nearly five thousand Alaskans. As you can imagine, it's a chilly place to call home. While southern states receive an inch or two of snow per year, flakes fall in Barrow every month of the year.

It is below zero degrees at least 160 days per year. That is nearly half the year with temperatures below zero, not just below freezing. Residents only experience 120 days in a calendar year with temperatures that rise above freezing.

On top of being cold and snowy, Barrow is also one of the cloudiest places on earth. It is completely overcast 50 percent of the year. People there rarely see temperatures rise above forty-five, and it has never risen above eighty degrees. Ever.

Here is where it can become depressing. From May 11 to August 1, the sun doesn't set. There is continuous light. However, the flip side is that the sun sets on November 18 and doesn't rise again until January 23. That is sixty-five days of darkness.

It should come as no surprise that in places above the Arctic Circle that experience lengthy seasons with no sunlight, depression rates often rise in the wintertime. In fact, the *American Journal of Psychiatry* discovered that winter is a drag for 20 percent of Americans. Even in Memphis, after a few winter days of dark clouds and freezing rain, people go into a funk.

A smaller fraction of Americans suffer from Seasonal Affective Disorder, which is a type of depression stemming from decreased sunlight. Nearly ten percent of Alaskans suffer from the disorder. Severe cases can be debilitating, even prompting thoughts of suicide.

Here is what I found so interesting, and this has become the inspiration of this book: there tends to be a peak season for suicide attempts in northern Alaska, and most of us would place our bets on it being the wintertime, when it is cold and dark.

But it's not.

Depression and suicide rates actually peak with increasing spring light. Locals have discovered that there is noticeable tension and difficulty when it comes to **reentry** into the light. The article ends with this statement, "The problem is reentry." One person said, "You don't have enough energy to make a plan before then. It's too much trouble. Once the light starts coming back, there's more energy, but reasoning is still off."[2]

Now, it's important to point out that this research wasn't focused on Barrow, but on the towns, cities, and villages in northern Alaska. I would not use the word *depressed* to describe the people of Barrow. My experience there gave me stories about the values that hold people together as they endure seasons of darkness as well as how they anticipate the reappearance of the sun.

Wherever we live, forms of darkness are often due to sin, but that is not always the case. Whether it is moral failure, guilt and shame, decades of apathy, paralyzing fear, greed, racism, depression, attachments, doubt, relational dysfunction, or grief, people everywhere are desperate for the good news of reentry into the light. This book takes people on this journey into greater forms of freedom.

In Christianity, the message of entry is something we all emphasize. Jesus entered the world, and in conversion we enter a covenant with him. The message of entry is needed. Jesus invited. People responded. They entered a relationship and a mission. One cannot argue with the fact that there are entry points.

However, one thing I have discovered as a disciple and pastor is how desperate people are for a message of reentry. Ordinary Christ-followers are often eager for reentry. I'm not referring to a loss of eternal status with God. I am referring to the many seasons of doubt, confusion, darkness, intentional sin, bondage to the past, severed relationships, job loss, and stress, which often paralyze us for a time. So, how do we reenter the light when we've been through the valleys, deserts, or wildernesses? How do we accept God's invitation to reenter the deep places of his heart and mission in this world? How do we move forward with God when we know the future will not be like the past because of changing circumstances?

This is why I went to Barrow. To learn from the community, because I'm convinced they have something to teach us all.

❧

I landed in Barrow around 11:00 A.M. I put on my toboggan (a warm knit cap), and we walked off the plane. I took my first breath in the cold air, and I could feel my nose hairs begin to freeze. *Maybe this is what death feels like*, I thought to myself. The tiny airport terminal was only a few feet away from the plane, and we walked in and stood by the baggage claim, which happened to be a garage door.

Before the quarter-mile walk to the hotel, I made sure my ski mask, gloves, and hat were on. I stepped outside and began to walk with my luggage. It was a few minutes past 11:00 A.M., and it was twilight. It would still be another week before this community would see the sun, but a haze—a glow—spread across the sky. It would be the equivalent of the final twenty or thirty minutes of daylight I usually experience in Memphis.

After settling into the hotel, I decided it was time to go eat lunch. After a brief conversation with the woman who ran the hotel I would call home for the next eleven days, she gave me directions to a restaurant a few blocks away. She made sure I understood her directions, because to get lost in those weather conditions could mean frostbite. Nearly every building I went into had a chart with temperatures and wind-chill numbers, and listed how many minutes you could last in the cold before exposed skin would begin to freeze.

As I walked the streets of Barrow, I felt like I was in a ghost town. The only vehicles on the icy roads were city trucks, taxicabs, and pizza delivery vehicles. Of course, no one was sitting on their porches sipping tea or smoking cigarettes.

After devouring a bacon cheeseburger and engaging in some good conversations with a few people at the restaurant about life on the northern slope, I started back to the hotel, and that led to my first encounter with death and death's friends.

I had been warned about polar bears from a variety of sources before my trip, and most places in Barrow had a poster on their walls reading BE ALERT for POLAR BEARS. The poster gave helpful information about the activity of polar bears throughout the seasons of the year, how to avoid problems, and what to do if a bear approaches. There were a lot of bullet points on the poster, but in the bottom right, under the section If a Bear Attacks, there were only two words: DEFEND YOURSELF! In other words, "You're going down, so just try to get a swing in."

I was walking down a quiet street, and with a ski mask on and a coat zipped up to the very top, my peripheral vision was basically gone. To my right, I heard the sound of something beginning to run at me. Its feet were moving fast and I could hear panting and a growl under its breath. With the little vision I had, I could tell it was white.

Some people would make the claim that a thirty-three-year-old man—dressed in a ski bib, with layers of clothes, a heavy coat, and ski boots—would be unable to duplicate the forty-yard dash he ran when he played high school football in Dallas. But I am here to tell you that you would be wrong. I was like the Road Runner from Looney Tunes. I had the form of Usain Bolt and the determination of Rudy.

After running twenty yards I turned around to see if I had created any distance between me and the man-hunting polar bear, and that's when I saw a beautiful, white, furry Samoyed dog tied to a leash in his front yard. Reality was, it was a big dog. For me that day, it was a polar bear.

∿

There is one conversation from Barrow that I will never forget. One day, I sat down with a local therapist, and I asked him about the difficulty some people have as they transition out of the lengthy season of darkness. He told me that occasionally, as the sun slowly returns, he feels some forms of depression rising in his heart. He went on to say that after a cold, frigid winter, you expect that the sun will bring change. However, when the sun reappears and peeks over the horizon for the first time in over two months, the conditions often get worse. The elements don't improve. It often gets colder, and the snow and ice continue to fall.

Has that ever been true in your own life?

Maybe you expected that when you surrendered your life to Jesus, things would change, but you soon discovered that many of the same elements that were with you before you entered life with Jesus were still nearby.

Maybe you came out of a season of intentional sin, and you hoped the light that was breaking into your life would drown out the darkness, but you had to learn how to avoid the elements that still play so loudly in our culture.

The process of *reentry* is vital for missionaries and soldiers who are returning home, inmates who are being released, young boys who are being set free from child slavery on the lakes of Ghana, and young girls experiencing freedom from sex trafficking. Reentry matters more than we may realize.

The best way to counter harsh elements is to embrace life in the light. And the invitation to thrive in the light is never ending. It keeps coming, like the waves of the ocean or the rising of the sun.

Join in its invitation.

You were made for it.

Notes

[1]Associated Press, "In Alaska, Darkness and Depression Descend," *New York Times*, December 18, 2005, http://www.nytimes.com/2005/12/18/national/in-alaska-darkness-and-depression-descend.html?_r=1.

[2]Ibid.

CHAPTER 2

Walking in the Dark

Our two boys share a room and, most nights, putting them to bed is quite the challenge. The comedian Jim Gaffigan says that putting your kids to bed becomes like a hostage negotiation . . . in reverse. Instead of negotiating for them to come out, you negotiate to keep them in.

"Listen, boys, if you stay in there and quit coming out, we will pay for all four years of college, and I'll pay the first three months of your mortgage when you buy a home one day."

The boys yell, "What about Incredible Pizza this Friday?"

"Yes, we will take you to Incredible Pizza. Just stay in there."

Most nights, they're awake because they don't want to miss out on life, but every once in a while, they are awake because they're afraid of the dark.

So, we have taught them to recite the command in Scripture that shows up more than any other command, "Do not be afraid." Reciting it is one thing. Allowing it to marinate until it has established itself in the center of your heart is another. Yet, we are learning.

Did you know that the books in the Bible that talk the most about darkness are also the books that talk the most about light?

It is as if God wants his people to know that where darkness exists, light is eager to break in. Light doesn't shy away from darkness. It never has. It never will.

For the most part, darkness is something to be feared, but sometimes darkness becomes the place where we meet with God. Before we go any further in a book discussing access and reentry into light, we need to pause to reflect on the function and activity of darkness. Most times, darkness represents evil; but sometimes it is the place where God revives a hurting heart.

Learning in the Dark

Which of your five senses do you treasure the most?

When I ask this question in group settings, most people quickly dismiss the sense of smell. Before they narrow it down to the one they treasure most, they eliminate the one they know they could live without. It's not that they don't enjoy the smell of a pot roast, fresh flowers, or the fireplace on a Christmas morning, but one could imagine living without smelling before they imagined living without physically seeing and touching the faces of loved ones.

There are always those who argue for taste, and it's not that losing vision or touch is enticing, but let's face it—we like to eat. And losing the ability to taste a steak, pork ribs, apple pie, or cheese biscuits from Red Lobster can throw lots of people into a minor depression.

Hands down, *sight* is the sense people argue for the most. They want vision. And we can all understand why, right? We want to see our children perform in plays and on ball fields. We want to watch movies with friends, and enjoy car rides through forests in the fall as leaves change colors.

Yet, we are inspired by those who hold on to hope and faith, even though they have suffered from blindness.

One of the great songwriters in the church was a woman born blind: Fanny J. Crosby.

About her blindness, Fanny said:

> It seemed intended by the blessed providence of God that I should be blind all my life, and I thank him for the dispensation. If perfect earthly sight were offered me tomorrow I would not accept it. I might not have sung hymns to the praise of God if I had been distracted by the beautiful and interesting things about me.
>
> If I had a choice, I would still choose to remain blind . . . for when I die, the first face I will ever see will be the face of my blessed Saviour.[1]

Most of us read that and think, "Wow. What faith! Good for her. But I still want to see."

Did you know that Jesus healed blindness more often than any other illness or disease? In fact, Jesus is the one who first introduces the healing of the blind in Scripture. Miraculous stories of restored vision aren't found in the Old Testament. It is a distinctive gift that Jesus brought into the world. I'm not suggesting that Jesus preferred blind people over the deaf, mute, or lame. I think most of the stories of blind people being healed also function to show how Jesus longs to open the eyes of our hearts to the deeper things of God.

At the end of Mark 10, Jesus encounters a blind man. Matthew and Luke also tell this story, but only Mark gives him a name. His name is Bartimaeus. By giving him a name, Mark gives him dignity. Most people referred to him as "that blind beggar over there." Mark names him.

When Jesus gets close to him, Bartimaeus begins yelling for him, and people tell the blind guy to shut up. Then, Jesus does a couple of things that sound quite odd. He asks the blind man to come to him. If you're Peter, there had to be the temptation to say, "Jesus, umm . . . I know you probably know this, but the guy is blind. He can't see. Why don't you go to him, instead of having him come to you?"

However, Jesus doesn't always heal people in ways you would expect. Just earlier, in Mark 7:33, Jesus healed a deaf and mute man by putting his fingers in the dude's ear, followed by spitting and touching the man's tongue. We only hope Jesus used Crest toothpaste, right?

If asking the man to come to him wasn't odd enough, the first thing Jesus says to him is in the form of a question, "What do you want me to do for you?" Again, if you're Peter or one of the apostles, it is obvious, right? The guy is blind. Clearly, the dude wants to see.

I love this question Jesus asks! In fact, it has worked its way into nearly every discipleship time and counseling session I have facilitated.

What do you want Jesus to do for you?

The brilliance of this question is that Jesus is eager for people to articulate what they want from God. It's not that Jesus is pretending to ask for orders like you would at Burger King or McDonald's, but he wants to hear you put into words the cry of your heart. Jesus wants us to articulate what it is we want of him.

Bartimaeus says, "My teacher, let me see again." Some translations leave off "again." But the Greek word *anablepō* is often used to refer to the blind regaining sight. Think about it; this means there was a time in Bartimaeus's life when he could see.

I don't know what would be more difficult. To have never been able to see, or to completely lose one's vision at some point in life.

There have been times in my life that I've made the same request Bartimaeus made.

"God, I want to see again. I've been distracted. I've been confused. I have strayed. I have lost sight of your will, your heart, and your mission. Let me see again."

And the more I read of God, the more I think there are few things God loves better than restoring sight to his people.

Can Darkness Be a Friend?

The thought of darkness and the inability to see the light sounds depressing. We aren't sure how we would exist. Imagine a life without watching Netflix, staring at a phone, and watching sunsets. How would we exist?

But maybe Fanny J. Crosby knew something we don't . . . that not being able to see, or sitting in darkness for a while, may be the key to opening our hearts to the greater things of God.

Can darkness be a friend?

Just a few years ago, I would have answered no to the question: *Can darkness be a friend*? No way!

Then two things happened:

1. My sister's death sent me into a lengthy season of darkness, and I am still discovering how God met me in the darkest places.
2. In 2014, Barbara Brown Taylor wrote a new book called *Learning to Walk in the Dark*.

The sudden death of my sister sent me into a season of doubt and confusion. I guess you could say I entered into a semi-faith crisis. It wasn't that I doubted the existence of God, but I had never been more confused about the intervention of God. Yet, I couldn't get past the truth and power of the incarnation and resurrection of Jesus. They anchored me. These two words became the primary convictions that kept me rooted. They wouldn't let me go. Jesus entered into human flesh to walk with it, in it, and for it. He rose from the grave to dismantle the powers of darkness (Col. 2:15), and to bring dead things to life. And what God did through and for Jesus, he does for us too.

I began working on this book in the spring of 2014, and Barbara Brown Taylor released her book shortly afterward. I was set on writing a book about how we need to flee darkness to thrive with God, and then she writes this book on why we should embrace darkness as the place to meet God. Honestly, she kind of made me mad; I wanted to kick her in the shin, because she was debunking my convictions behind this book.

I have a lot of respect for Barbara Brown Taylor. In fact, in seminary, my classmates and I became huge fans. We could only call her by her full name, though. *Barbara* seemed disrespectful. One friend attempted to call her *BBT*, and he almost got stoned. *Mrs. Taylor* didn't seem fitting either. She has always been Barbara Brown Taylor to us. Our preaching professors had us listen to her in college. I've heard very few preachers who care more for the Bible than she does. She treats each sermon as if it is her very last, carefully handling each passage with great precision and care. For her, it is a craft. So, if she thought darkness was a good idea to write about, I thought I'd better check out why.

At a young age, we are taught to eliminate darkness. Yet, Barbara Brown Taylor argues, "New life starts in the dark. Whether it is a seed in the ground, a baby in the womb, or Jesus in the tomb, it starts in the dark."[2] And she is right. I didn't want her to be right, but she's right. "How do we develop the courage to walk in the dark if we are never asked to practice?"[3]

Until Jesus returns to set the world right, the question lives on: *When is darkness evil and when is it of God?*

There are over one hundred references to darkness in Scripture, and many of them are in the context of sin, evil, conflict, tension, and how darkness wants to possess and override a heart. But occasionally, darkness shows up in Scripture as a gift.

Surprisingly, darkness isn't called evil or referred to as evil in Genesis 1–2. In fact, it almost serves as a prelude to a deep truth: *new life always begins in the dark.*

Sometimes God puts out our light in order to teach us how to function better. God-induced darkness may just be God's way of slowing you down, releasing you from unnecessary burdens, and creating an atmosphere where he can slowly examine and transform your heart into something that reflects his divine nature.

In the sixteenth century, Saint John of the Cross wrote a poem that has come to be called "Dark Night of the Soul." He describes the difficult invasion of God's grace that penetrates deep into our souls. It pries open our hearts to God's desire to lay us bare. The ultimate test is this: if we immediately run from this "dark night of the soul," we may miss out on God. You see, ancient mystics used to teach that "dark nights" are not problems to be avoided, but rather opportunities to be embraced.

This aligns with many of the narratives and experiences we discover in Scripture. Prior to some of God's most remarkable work in Scripture, we read about caves, prison cells, wombs, and tombs.

I bet you have done some cave time before too. I know I have. Cave times are seasons when you have been betrayed, wrongly treated, or left alone. Cave times are also periods of deep reflection, either because of sin and weakness, or because of a prompting for your heart to grow stronger.

Yet, without cave time or prison cells, the psalms and a few of Paul's letters wouldn't have been given to us as gifts revealing that God doesn't leave us alone in our imprisonment, oppression, and darkness.

~

I had a friend, Kyle, join me for the second half of the trip to Barrow. He is an artist who traveled with me as a videographer to shoot testimonies and stories, and to get footage of this adventure. But the first five days in Barrow, I was alone. I found myself working ten to twelve hours a day. My goal was to make as many connections as possible before Kyle arrived, so testimonies would already be scheduled to shoot. With the help of two pastors, the local high school principal, a librarian at the city library, and a radio talk show host, I began making friends and hearing stories.

Within the first few minutes of my arrival at the hotel, there was a knock on the door. A local pastor I had connected with on Facebook came by to welcome me to Barrow. With a smile on his face, he said, "I googled you, and I discovered you are a real person." After laughing, I asked, "What does that mean? Opposed to what?"

He said he'd found our church's website, had listened to some of my sermons, and he found links to the first book I wrote, *Scarred Faith*.

I did not go to Barrow to promote my first book or to speak at places, but that local Barrow pastor connected me to a few places where I would speak over the next couple of days. Each opportunity opened doors for me to connect with new friends and to hear their amazing stories.

I spoke at a local Baptist church for a recovery meeting, an Assembly of God church for a Sunday-night activity, a book club at the city library, and a radio show on the only radio station on the northern slope.

When the local high school heard an author was in town, they asked if I would be willing to speak to the entire student body the following afternoon. They asked me to talk about *Scarred Faith*. I was open to it, but I first wanted them to know that the book deals a lot with Jesus, hope, and resurrection. I wasn't sure if there would be any parameters set for me. The response was, "Say whatever you want. Just don't give an altar call at the end." Deal. I had a blast!

For five days, I ventured as much as I could throughout the town to meet people, ask questions, and to specifically hear what disciplines and rhythms help energize a heart and community through harsh winters. Yet, even though I met with people for half a day, that meant for the other half of the day, I was alone.

I don't mind being alone, though I'm a people-person (I'm a seven on the enneagram). But to be alone in an unfamiliar place is not something on my bucket list. I was still in the United States of America, but I was 3,421 miles from home. Strangely, I felt more at home in Lusaka, Zambia, than I did in Barrow. Lusaka had Kentucky Fried Chicken and fancy steak houses, but Barrow only had locally owned restaurants; it's part of what makes the town so unique.

If you are alone in an unfamiliar place, you could take walks, go shopping, or do what we do best—surf the Internet. But with weather thirty degrees below zero, you're encouraged to not be outside longer than fifteen minutes, so shopping wasn't an option, and the Internet connection was the equivalent of 1998 dial-up.

Over the first five days, I found myself going into a funk. My energy level was low. So, as I asked God to sustain me, I felt invited to rediscover Jesus as both the light of my life and the light of the world. Each day, I read through a Gospel. The first day—Matthew. Second day—Mark. Day 3—Luke. And day 4—John. Diving into the life and ministry of Jesus in the context I was in began opening me up to fresh aspects of God's heart and mission in the world. The eighteen references to "darkness" and thirty-six references to "light" in the Gospels jumped off the page every time I came across them.

Darkness Can Be a Friend

I know darkness is often referred to as evil. There are just over one hundred references to darkness in Scripture, and most of them are in the context of evil, conflict, and tension between darkness and light.

Today, many people suffer from nyctophobia, which is an extreme fear of darkness. The word itself—nyctophobia—comes from Nyx, one of the earliest and scariest gods of the Greeks. She was the daughter of Chaos, and chaos is exactly what people thought about the dark. Today, we have night-lights, and we leave at least one lamp on while we sleep. We turn on the light and crack the door so light can come in.

At the Memphis Zoo, there is a room called "Animals of the Night." It's dark. It's a room with bats, mice, and porcupines. There are animals that fit the definition of cute, and then there are the animals of the night. There are benches outside the exhibit, and they are constantly occupied by mothers, children, and others who patiently wait for their family and friends to go through the dark place without them. I know this, because I see them, and because it is where my wife waits on us.

Here is what I have learned in my life and ministry: sometimes God puts out your light so he can teach you how to function better. If you're in sin, God wants you to know how dark it is, so you'll crave him. When Jesus tells the story of the prodigal son, he says, "When he came to his senses." The younger brother had to be immersed in the mess of life—literally, all five of his senses were engaged in the life of pigs—in order to recognize the greater life he had with his father.

I've also learned that there can be God-induced darkness. It's not evil; it's God slowing you down. It's God eager to teach you something. It's God eager to reveal himself and to grow your heart.

New life always begins in the dark!

Seeds in the ground, baby in the womb, and Jesus in the tomb. From darkness comes new creation and new life.

In Genesis 1, God called light out of darkness, and it has become the continuous act of God throughout the history of the world.

You may feel you're in a dark season right now, yet I encourage you to cling to the words of Theodore Roethke, "In a dark time, the eye begins to see."[4]

Sometimes, God calls us out of darkness.

Sometimes, God call us to rest in it.

And sometimes, God calls us to walk through it.

Walking in the dark, with God, is not a bad place to be.

Notes

[1]"Faith Hall of Fame: Frances Jane van Alystyne (Fanny Crosby) 1820–1915 Hymn Writer," European-American Evangelistic Crusades, accessed February 14, 2017, http://www.eaec.org/faithhallfame/fanny_crosby.htm.

[2]Barbara Brown Taylor, *Learning to Walk in the Dark* (New York: HarperOne, 2014), 129.

[3]Ibid., 37.

[4]Theodore Roethke, "In a Dark Time," *The Collected Poems of Theodore Roethke* (New York: Doubleday, 1961), 239.

PART 1

REENTRY

They are everywhere in our home. Though Kayci and I attempt to keep them in one confined room, I have found them in couch cushions, in the bathtub, under beds, on the kitchen cabinet, and even in the dog's mouth. It has become the main reason I don't walk barefoot in the house. The last time I stepped on one, it left a bone bruise for days.

Legos.

My youngest son, Noah, is fascinated by them. It is the first thing he wants to do when he comes home from school. Lego Star Wars sets, Lego Jurassic World, Lego trains, Lego ball fields . . . it doesn't matter. He wants to build, and he is really good at it.

One thing I've learned while living in a smaller home with two young boys and a hyper dog is that it doesn't take long to destroy something. There have been days we have spent two hours building a Lego set, and it can come tumbling down with one roll of a bas-ketball, one misstep, or one door left open for the dog to run in.

Sounds like life too, right? In a short time—sometimes only seconds—life can change forever. One phone call. One medical test. One flirtatious moment. One drink. One lie. We can spend years building a career, a marriage, a reputation, and a plan, and in a moment, it can come tumbling down.

In all the weddings that I've ever performed, I've never had someone say, "I hope we just make it to year seventeen." I've yet to sit with a college graduate who said, "I hope I'm clinically depressed and overcome by anxiety by thirty-seven." I've never heard a third grader express a dream of becoming a heroin addict.

Much like the seasons of the year, we have seasons in life too. And often we find ourselves in transitions we never asked to be in. It makes you wonder, do we choose transitions, or do they choose us?

So, if transitions and shifts in life are inevitable, what do we do to prepare for them? Can we plan ahead, and if so, how? If we are currently in a place of uncertainty, how do we navigate our way through it? What role does God play in navigating, and what are the things God expects us to do?

Faith Is More than What You Know

Faith, at its best, is not simply about what you know, but what you do with what you know. Faith—deep faith—is about movement. We move with what we know to be true.

Yet here is the challenge, especially in Western Christianity. We have often reduced faith as movement into a conversion moment, rather than a radically transformed life. The focus has been on responding to God's invitation into salvation, while failing to emphasize how God continues to invite us into his heart and mission. The God who invites us into conversion is the same one who invites us from conversion moments into meaningful life. Put another way, the focus of what God has accomplished through the death, burial, and resurrection of Jesus is not only what we are saved from, but also what we are saved into. Movement into God's salvation now becomes movement alongside our God who has saved us.

This is why the Bible doesn't talk about relationship with Jesus as life insurance, fire insurance, a safety net, or a get-out-of-hell-free card. Instead, we are bombarded by language of walking and living with Jesus. God, in his love and faithfulness, both invites and expects movement.

My journey with this theme of reentry has taught me that life with Christ is about movement; however, it is anything but a straight road with zero traffic and cruise control. There are twists, turns, potholes, speed bumps, construction zones, obstacles, elements, and times when we get rerouted.

I think I'm at my worst as a Christian when I get stuck in traffic. It's as if the fruit of the Spirit just up and leaves my body. All that love-joy-peace-patience-kindness-gentleness stuff goes out the window . . . as does my witness to Jesus.

My wife and I moved to Memphis late in the spring of 2008. Since then, we have traveled back to Texas to visit family a few times a year. And if you have driven on I-40 between Memphis and Little Rock, you know there is always a chance that road construction will lead to standstills.

I thought road construction could never get any worse than the stretch between Memphis and Little Rock—until I drove I-35 between Fort Worth and Austin. It made the drive between Little Rock and Memphis seem like a cakewalk.

We had just left a family vacation in San Antonio, and we needed to make the twelve-hour drive back to Memphis for me to preach the next morning. Then, I-35 happened.

After traveling a whopping distance of 0.9 miles in a couple of hours, I had turned into someone I never wanted to become. I was gripping the wheel, hitting the wheel, raising my voice at drivers who either cut me off or failed to move up in traffic because they were catching up on Facebook while stopped.

It got so bad that, at one point, my boys talked to my wife about me. We were in a small Honda Civic Hybrid, so they were only two feet behind me, but they still talked to Kayci about me . . . not to me. I could hear everything they were saying, but they were too afraid to talk to me. So they asked her, "Mom, is Dad okay? Is he going to be all right?"

Kayci answered, "He is going to be okay. Your dad just needs to spend some time with Jesus for a minute." Then she looked at me, "Don't you, honey?"

Spend time with Jesus? Honey?

I snapped back, "Don't 'honey' me. Your momma needs to spend time with Jesus. I'm fine. I'm perfectly fine."

That's when I quickly exited to get some comfort food. When I get stuck in traffic because of road construction, food from gas stations makes me feel better about myself. Pregnant women aren't the only ones who need comfort food; so do grown men who get stuck in traffic. I bought Funyuns, hot tamales, spicy beef jerky, a Twix, a Red Bull, and some squirt cheese. Yum! Does the body good! (My wife also vowed that there would be no kissing for at least twenty-four hours for two reasons: because of my attitude, and because of what the food I was devouring would do to my body.)

After being rerouted, we were back on the road, and in case you are wondering, I did make it back in time to preach.

Can you think of a time when your day was heavily impacted by traffic or road construction? Some of you deal with it every day. In fact, you know it will be there, so you plan ahead for it.

Can you identify the moments in life when you have been knocked off course, either by sin, or because of circumstances? What changed? What impact did it have on your pace in life? Were you able to find your way back? Have you found your way back?

∿

I was only in Barrow one Sunday. I was invited to speak at a Baptist church in the morning and an Assemblies of God church that night. That evening, after a time of praise, I was asked to speak about my book *Scarred Faith*, and to also share with the church why I had chosen to visit Barrow. On the back row sat a woman who looked distressed, almost like she was wrestling in her spirit with whether to stay or leave. I spoke about wounds and scars. Wounds seem to be a natural part of life. However, scars are healed wounds. And every scar we bear has a story that goes with it. There is not a scar on our body that we don't know the story that goes with it. The problem in life is when we don't allow wounds to become scars. We constantly pick at them, keeping them exposed and vulnerable to infection. We have physical, social, psychological, and emotional wounds and scars.

As I shared this image, the woman on the back row began to cry. She wasn't wailing; in fact, I was probably the only one who could see her. I didn't know what to do, so I just continued speaking.

I went on to talk about my research about darkness, light, and the challenge of reentry. The crowd nodded their heads in agreement. I was very careful in how I talked about depression and darkness, because I had come to Barrow to learn, not to project ideas on people.

I went on to share about entry and reentry, and I used the story of Peter to talk about it. It was around that time that I came across the times in Peter's life when he left boats for Jesus. It didn't just happen once. It kept happening throughout the Gospels. Each time

Peter left a boat for Jesus was an invitation into deeper faith. The first one was to enter into an adventure with Jesus. We can call it his conversion. But boats keep showing up, Peter keeps getting in them, and Jesus keeps inviting him to jump out.

After the worship service, this woman stayed around to talk with me. In tears, she shared how she didn't want to come, but a friend told her an author was in town who had written a book about pain, suffering, and faith. On the way to church, she clutched the steering wheel and pulled over two different times in an effort to turn around. Yet, she kept feeling as if God wanted her there. She went on to share about some of the wounds and scars in her own life, and then proceeded to tell me how she connected with the second story I told about Peter leaving a boat for Jesus. It's the time the disciples got caught in the storm. That described her life. Some storms had knocked her off course, and she was trying to find her way back. Not back to salvation in Jesus, but back to adventurous, joyous faith.

Walking with Jesus involves invitation and response. His invitation. Our response. And responding to his invitation may just be exactly what you need as you navigate your way through the shifts and transitions in life.

When we think of the function of boats in our culture, we think of recreation, fishing, sailing, and enjoyment. In the first century, boats were about transportation, vocation, and survival. In the Gospels, boats created obstacles, illusions of safety, and more importantly, they were the setting of vital decisions made to follow Jesus.

The next three chapters will unpack three of these encounters between Jesus and Peter, and I bet if you take the stories seriously, you'll find yourself in them too.

CHAPTER 3

Captured Alive

Once a year, we travel a few hours from Memphis into Arkansas to spend a couple of days at Heber Springs. It's the second-clearest lake in the United States. We notice the beauty, but we go for the fun.

In the summer of 2015, our friends the Parsons went with us. After a few hours on the boat, my boys (seven and five at the time), decided they wanted to go jump off the cliffs. There are two sets of cliffs that are near each other at Heber Springs. One set is for amateurs. The other set is for crazy people.

My goal was to take my boys to the smaller cliffs, jump off a few times, and then leave without them seeing the much taller ones. But after a few jumps off the ten-foot rocks, my boys spotted the others. And they began to beg like they do when they see a can of Pringles at the store.

My attempts at talking them out of it weren't working. Call me lazy if you want, but I didn't want to walk all the way over to the higher cliffs, only to stand on the edge and then have them chicken out. Cliffs that are thirty to thirty-five feet high may not look tall from a distance, but when you stand on the top of one, all of a sudden you feel like you're on Mount Everest.

Confession time: I knew an adult needed to jump in before they did to make sure they would be safe. And what I didn't want to do was to jump in, resurface, and have them back out.

Together with the Parsons, we walked to the edge of the big cliffs. I looked at my boys to see their initial reaction, and, surprising to me, they were ready to jump. I looked at Patrick Parson—who is an elder at our church—and said, "Bro, God called you to be a shepherd to your sheep. I think you should jump in first to lead the way. The sheep need to follow their fearless shepherd."

Patrick wasn't buying the theological argument I was making. Apparently the shepherd/sheep metaphor breaks down in some areas of life.

I jumped in first, and resurfaced just in time to hear splashes on my right and on my left. I heard Kayci yell, "Truitt is on your right and Noah is on your left!"

After a few more jumps, we left to eat some burgers and fries.

The more I study Jesus, the more I see that faith is a great adventure. It is often a risk, a leap. It is coming to the edge, looking fear in the face, and choosing to jump anyway.

A Leap of Faith

When we first meet Peter in Luke 5, he is fishing. It was his job. It was his livelihood.

I'm sure fishing jokes existed then like they do now.

Such as the mother who gave her daughter advice: Cook a man a fish and you feed him for a day. But teach a man to fish and you get rid of him for the whole weekend.

Or maybe you heard about the small-town doctor who was famous in the area for always catching large fish. One day while he was on one of his frequent fishing trips he got a call that a woman at a neighboring farm was giving birth. He rushed to her aid and delivered a healthy baby boy. The farmer had nothing to weigh the baby with, so the doctor used his fishing scales. The baby weighed 21 lb. 13 oz.

When Jesus first meets Peter in Luke, Peter has just come in from a long night of fishing, and he was completely empty-handed. He had caught nothing!

There were two boats, and Jesus decided to get in one. In those days, boats were probably twenty to thirty feet in length. Not massive. Not terribly small either.

Two things happen when Jesus gets into this boat:

- Jesus got away from the crowd so he could teach them. They were pressing in on him, so he created a little distance. And in this moment, all of the introverts give out a collective "Amen!"
- Jesus entered into Peter's world. This is significant, and I think we often miss it. Jesus willingly stepped into Peter's world before he asked Peter to step into his. Jesus does the same for us. Not only does he invite us into his life, but he injects himself into ours. He enters into our space, our time, our circumstances in order to reveal himself as God-with-us.

After teaching, Jesus told Peter to go back out to fish again. Jesus was very specific about this. His words weren't just to go out and fish, but to go out into deep waters to fish. Jesus's invitation is always into deeper waters. For his followers, it becomes a matter of obedience. Will we listen to his voice or not?

However, Peter had already clocked out. His wife had food on the table. The sun was setting. And Jesus, who wasn't a professional fisherman, tells a professional fisherman how to do his job. Don't you hate it when people who don't do what you do attempt to tell you how to do what it is you do?

Peter obeyed, and they caught so many fish that their boats began to sink and their nets began to break. Something miraculous was happening. And in that moment, Peter left the miracle to move into the presence of the miracle worker.

Peter's response was to fall at the feet of Jesus and say, "Go away from me, Lord, for I am a sinful man!" (Luke 5:8). Peter knew he was in the presence of greatness. Here is the reality: it is dangerous to be a sinner in the presence of God. But maybe not for the reasons you think.

I do believe in hell, evil, Satan, and the powers of darkness. Yet Jesus's strategy to draw Peter into a relationship wasn't to begin with how evil and sinful Peter was, but with how powerful and miraculous God is. Jesus searches for sinners, not to affirm them in their rebellion, but to transform them into God's likeness.

Jesus didn't have to use words to convict Peter of his sins. Instead he demonstrated his power, and mercy flowed. When Jesus did speak, here's what he said: "Do not be afraid; from now on *you will be catching people*" (v. 10—emphasis mine).

Matthew and Mark have Jesus saying, "From now on you will be fishers of men," but Luke has Jesus saying something just a little bit different.

In the Greek, the word for "catching people" is *zogreō*, which literally means being captured alive. This isn't an invitation to kidnap. It is an invitation to join in God's initiative to capture people from head to toe. It is to invite them into a relationship in which they are all in. Not ankle-deep. Not knee-deep. Not neck-deep. But all in. Captured alive!

It seems to be easy to want Jesus as a caregiver, but he is interested in being so much more.

Peter's response (along with others) was to leave everything and follow Jesus. Sometimes dropping nets and leaving the boat means we leave vocations too, but it doesn't always mean that.

However, it does mean a shift in allegiance. It's a new way of life. We leave the old behind, and we enter into something fresh.

When it comes to life with Jesus, there has to be an entry. There cannot be reentry into life or light until there has been entry. Decisions have to be made for Christ. You may not have an elaborate testimony that will ever make it on iamsecond.com. You may not be the prodigal son or daughter who squandered wealth on wild living. Yet at some point we must realize we are sinners who need Jesus. Many people want the benefits that flow from God without ever making the decision to step into an everlasting commitment with him.

God invites us to the edge. And he invites us to jump.

Leave the boat behind. Because there is a relationship to pursue.

A fire has been lit.

The old has gone.

The new has come.

The boats are left behind.

And the adventure begins.

Jesus Isn't Always Safe

I attended a church camp in high school, and early one morning, around 1:00 A.M. to be exact, someone decided they wanted to be baptized right then, and they wanted me to do it. I come from a faith tradition that practices baptism by immersion. A few of us piled into a van and drove down to the river. As we approached the water, the headlights shone down into the water where people were often baptized, and that's when we saw a couple of water moccasins swim away into the deeper parts of the river. In that moment, I began to question everything I knew about immersion. I became envious of some of my friends who practice sprinkling and pouring.

Then it hit me: the Bible says nothing about someone who has to have his or her hands on the person wanting to be baptized. I was tempted to just tell the guy to get in the water, and whenever he saw my hand make a motion down, he could go down in the water. At that point, he was free to stay down there with Jesus as long as he wanted, and to come up when he felt alive and ready.

To me, it seemed the safest route to take. After all, what better place to die than under water with Jesus, right?

But one thing I've discovered the more I spend time with Jesus is this: confessing Jesus as Lord and choosing to be baptized isn't about being safe. In fact, it is risky. It is dangerous. It is about full allegiance to a new kingdom and a new way.

Covenant is risky business. Jesus doesn't invite you into it to simply save you from hell, but to give you a new sense of purpose and identity in this world.

Jesus knew this, because Jesus lived this. Do you remember where Jesus was baptized?

It was the Jordan River.

The Jordan is one of the fastest-flowing rivers in the world. It begins at the base of Mount Hermon, which is around 1,500 feet above sea level. The river flows for two hundred miles, and it empties into the Dead Sea, which is roughly 1,500 below sea level. Consider the difference, and I will trust that you know how gravity works. If you aren't sure, just know that it is a fast-flowing river.

The Jordan River isn't very wide, yet it is very dangerous. Many in the ancient world considered rivers and the sea to be sacred. They thought that gods owned and ran them. They weren't to be messed with.

You see, throughout Scripture, the Jordan River was a place of salvation and deliverance, but it was often an obstacle to overcome.

To enter the Jordan River took courage, balance, and bravery. And it was the river where Jesus was baptized. The river symbolized the journey to the cross. There would be obstacles, yet if God could lift him out of the Jordan in baptism, God could lift him above every obstacle that was to come. And what God did for Jesus, he's eager to do for you too.

Learning from the Jordan River

The Jordan River is mentioned around two hundred times in Scripture. Seventy of them are in a book called Joshua. Here is what you need to know about Joshua: it is a book that highlights God's covenant keeping, and there is also some fighting and dying. Well, actually, there is a lot of fighting and dying. It is kind of like 24; in the end, there may be just one survivor. Don't get attached to a character, because it probably won't work out for them in the end.

Joshua ends like an obituary in the newspaper. It is a list of people who died. What a way to end a book in the Bible, right?

But earlier in the book, the obstacle wasn't an enemy to fight, but a river to cross.

3:8: You are the one who shall command the priests who bear the ark of the covenant, "When you come to the edge of the waters of the Jordan, *you shall stand still* in the Jordan."

3:13: When the soles of the feet of the priests who bear the ark of the LORD, the Lord of all the earth, *rest in the waters* of the Jordan, the waters of the Jordan flowing from above shall be cut off; they shall stand in a single heap.

3:15–16: Now the Jordan overflows all its banks throughout the time of harvest. So when those who bore the ark had come to the Jordan, *and the feet of the priests bearing the ark were dipped in the edge of the water*, the waters flowing from above stood still, rising up in a single heap far off at Adam, the city that is

beside Zarethan, while those flowing toward the sea of
the Arabah, the Dead Sea, were wholly cut off. Then the
people crossed over opposite Jericho. (Emphasis added)

Before God parted the river, he asked them to step in it. This
wasn't a show to be watched, but a partnership to be entered into.
God did the amazing, but not without asking for radical trust.
Stepping into the Jordan was a step of faith. They stepped in, God
performed his wonders, and God's covenant was confirmed. The
people of God moved into a new land.

Living into Freedom

But Joshua isn't about people being made free. It doesn't end that
way. The book ends by asking, "What does freedom mean?" Or,
"What kind of life are freed people supposed to live?"

You see, in Joshua 23:1 we read this, "A long time afterward."
Years went by. The people had *settled* into a new land.

And the words *settled* and *freedom* can often do weird things
to us.

It can give us a deep appreciation for the gift of freedom.
However, it can sometimes pave the way for forms of complacency,
apathy, and entitlement to creep in and take over.

When free people forget why they have been set free, all hell
can break loose within a heart, a family, a community, and even
in a nation.

Lessons from Memphis

During my first couple of years in Memphis, I asked God to help
me get to know my new city. The prayer of my heart was to learn
to love Memphis as God does, but in order to do that, I needed to
get to know the city. So I found myself doing ride-alongs with the
fire department and with police officers. Those were experiences
I'll never forget.

One night, my friend Patrick—yes, the same Patrick I mentioned earlier in this chapter—was going to take me out for a night of getting to know Memphis. As a Memphis police officer, he knows the city very well, and by the grace of God, his heart has not grown calloused to the pain and brokenness he sees on the job.

He had a few guys he needed to visit anyway, so he invited me to tag along. Since he was off duty, he asked if I could take my truck. It wasn't just any truck. It was my 1995 Ford Ranger. She was born into our family in 1995 when my dad bought her brand-new. When I went to college, he sold it to me. Up until October 2012, she existed as a member of the Ross clan. She made it seventeen years and over 230,000 miles before dying on I-75 in Dallas while taking one of my good friends to the airport. But we don't talk about that.

Our first stop was to visit a guy who had a few warrants out for him. However, he was working with the cops to solve a few cases to reduce his sentence. When I say a few cases, within a few weeks this guy had solved three murders and was giving valuable tips of specific locations where motorcycles and pills would soon be stolen. This guy was good. Much like Raymond Reddington from the hit show *The Blacklist*.

While visiting with him, we told stories and shared some laughs. Then I told him that we were going to be driving my truck around the rest of the evening and that we were going to be in some pretty rough places. I asked him if my truck was going to be safe.

He looked at my truck and then he looked at me. Looked at my truck again. And then looked at me. Then he said, "Pastor, I don't want to hurt your feelings, but ain't nobody gonna touch your truck." We laughed. Then he followed that up with, "You can leave the truck unlocked, and nobody is going to touch your truck. Now, if you leave your wallet in the seat, someone will take your wallet, but they won't mess with this truck."

Toward the end of the conversation I asked him a more serious question. You see, for over 66 percent of the inmates at 201 Poplar (the infamous jail in Memphis), this is at least their sixth time to be in it.

My question to my friend that night was this: "Why would guys, after being set free, choose to make choices that would put them right back in bondage?"

He paused for a few moments before saying something I'll never forget: "Josh, I guess when it comes down to it, a lot of my friends don't know how to be free."

We don't know how to be free.

And after I thought about that statement, I wanted to say, "A lot of people I preach in front of week in and week out don't know how to be free either."

The Need for Entry

I think Joshua attempted to end his life reminding the people they weren't set free just to settle; they were set free in order to deeply live into their freedom. And there is a big difference between the two.

In Joshua 24, he gathered all the tribes and called forward the leaders. He had one final message, and what he took the time to do was recount the story of God. He walked them through what God had done.

But here is what I think is so important—this was more than a history lesson. Joshua was doing more than giving them a story to remember; he was giving them a story to live into. If I am not careful, I can decide that I am really much happier reading my Bible than I am entering into what God is doing in my own time and place, since shutting the book to go outside will involve the very great risk of taking part in stories that are still taking shape. But the written word—or in Joshua's case, the spoken word—was meant to become the living word.

You see, the book of Joshua was about *entering* into a new land, but it was also about reminding people that God will continue to invite his people to live into that freedom. That is what his covenant reminds us of. It doesn't just invite us once. Once we have entered into one place, it keeps inviting us to deeper places. And this is a gift!

Joshua, and Peter in Luke 5, knew that there would be seasons of darkness and even unfaithfulness, yet *reentry* into the freedom of God would still be available, because *entry* has been made available. That is exactly what the story of God continually reminds us of: what God did through Jesus to give us access into relationship with him is available to us all. It invites. We respond.

And this *entry* is about being ushered into a movement.

CHAPTER 4

When Grief Walks

Have you ever found yourself in a storm, and it seemed like Jesus was miles away?

As a pastor, I have performed numerous weddings and funerals. There have been some unforgettable moments. I'll never forget when my best friend put lighter fluid on his brother's unity candle. I still don't know how the bride didn't catch on fire when it burst into flames. Sadly, I once did a funeral for a woman who died from abuse. The entire family was highly dysfunctional, as bad as I've ever seen. In fact, the mother asked us to play Eminem and Rihanna's song about domestic abuse, *Love the Way You Lie*. I was so glad that our sound system broke just hours before the funeral. That was definitely an act of divine intervention.

I've had moments of seeing marriages crumble in front of me. I've had friends die of drug overdoses. I've had to be the one to tell friends and church members the tragic news of the loss of a son, a father, and other loved ones. I've been one of the first ones on the scene when friends took their own lives. Death and pain come in all different shapes and forms. And it really doesn't matter how prepared you are for it. Death stings.

When grief hits us, it moves in to stay. Grief isn't an occasional visitor or a monthly dinner guest. Grief establishes residence. Grief enters into the picture because of death, but that's not the only time it intrudes. Grief is about deep loss, and that can come in many different forms. Grief lingers. It doesn't go away. Sure, it takes on new shapes and sizes over time, but it sticks around.

While walking the journey with grief, it is good to know that God is not only the One who desires to lift you out of a pit, but he is also the One who is willing to get down in a pit with you. When you are at your lowest, you should take heart that God's grace can extend lower than your lowest low.

Grief is like the waves of the ocean. And it's like we are just along for the ride.

Permission to Mourn

Did you know there are two specific occasions in the Bible when Jesus weeps?

The first is when Lazarus died in Bethany. Some may know it as the shortest verse in the Bible, "Jesus wept" (John 11:35). He wept over a dead body, and he was minutes away from bringing it back to life. Jesus willingly stepped into the world of the other mourners who had gathered. Jesus knew something wasn't right with this death, and he knew something wasn't right with the world. And he wept over it and for it.

The second time Jesus wept was over a city. "As he came near and saw the city, he wept over it" (Luke 19:41). He wept over a city, knowing he was within a few days of dying for the very people who lived there. Jesus believed people—and Jerusalem—were worth crying over, and worth dying for.

One of the first statements out of Jesus's mouth when he launched his public ministry was this: "Blessed are those who mourn, for they will be comforted" (Matt. 5:4).

It has happened too many times to count. I will meet with people in my office, over breakfast, lunch, or coffee, and they will begin to share a hurt, pain, or form of brokenness. And occasionally—the person's age or gender doesn't matter—they will begin to cry.

Every single time except once, whoever it is that has gotten choked up in front me begins to apologize the moment they begin to weep.

What is it about crying that makes us feel like we have to apologize?

What is it about mourning and grief that makes us feel uncomfortable, embarrassed, and weak?

In their book *Heaven on Earth*, my good friends Josh Graves and Chris Seidman write, "Mourning is about a grief that compels one to act. . . . Mourning means you have a deep awareness of just how messed up things really are from the way things should be. In mourning, you are as close to God as you'll ever be."[1]

Mourning is a gift from God to release from the body that which does not belong. It is an ache that is a reminder that some things in our lives, and things in the world, are not as they should be.

One of the most memorable miracles of Jesus came in a time of great loss. Let's set the stage.

Wanting the Calm; Getting the Storm

Boats keep showing up in the Gospels. Peter keeps getting in them, and Jesus keeps inviting him to get out of them.

Matthew 14 begins with the tragic news that John the Baptist (Jesus's cousin) had been beheaded. And like many people when they first get the news of a devastating loss, Jesus wanted to go to a place where he could be alone.

"Now when Jesus heard this, he withdrew from there in a boat to a deserted place by himself" (Matt. 14:13).

You've been there before, right? The word comes of a tragedy. You want to get alone.

Alone so you can breathe.

Alone so you can release whatever emotion you're feeling.

Alone so you don't have to answer a million questions.

He withdrew. He escaped. He wanted some alone time.

But then he looks up, and here come a few people. Well . . . maybe more than a few. Thousands of them. Walking. Running.

In Jesus's moment of deep loss and grief, we are told, "He had compassion for them" (Matt. 14:14).

He healed their sick.

And then he fed thousands of them.

It is the only miracle in Jesus's public ministry that is mentioned in all four Gospels, and it comes from a place of deep sorrow and loss. Some of God's best work comes in our brokenness. God can use grieving, desperate, burdened, sorrow-filled people to accomplish his purposes. What God did in and through Jesus that day, he still does in and through us today.

But here is where the story gets wild.

Jesus told his disciples to get into a boat. Actually, we are told, "He made the disciples get into the boat" (Matt. 14:22). Stomachs full of bread and fish, and they get into a boat.

The boat ends up in the middle of a lake, and a storm comes in, while Jesus goes in the opposite direction to go up on a mountain to pray. The boat was being "battered by the waves" (v. 24). It's a word that literally means "tortured." Even if you aren't easily prone to motion sickness, this doesn't sound appealing. This alone is why some people don't take cruises. When you're in a car and you begin to feel carsick, you can pull over, walk around, and catch your breath. But when you're in a boat, and the waves hit, there is nothing you can do. Nothing!

Here's the irony: it was evening, Jesus was praying.

They were struggling, and Jesus kept praying.

Hours went by. The waves kept coming. And Jesus kept praying.

I find it strange that Jesus didn't leave his prayer time the moment they began to struggle. He didn't abandon his moment to pour out his grief to his Father because waves were intensifying.

So, have you ever found yourself in a storm, and it seemed like Jesus was miles away?

It was the fourth watch of the night (which would have been between 3:00 and 6:00 A.M.) before Jesus began making his way to them. And let's just say . . . Jesus chose an unconventional route. He walked on the water.

Now, for those of you who are wired as skeptics, this is the point that it can become easy to dismiss the story, because this sounds impossible. But hang with me.

In this moment, we learn two things about the heart and mission of Jesus:

1. He was eager to be in the presence of his Father . . . alone!
2. He was eager to be present with his disciples in their distress.

Sometimes it is difficult to comprehend how Jesus is present in storms and distress. These are the moments that can shake us to the core. The storms of life can lead us to believe that we are alone, isolated, and vulnerable. It's the place where identity can be shaken, the truths we've been taught seem fragile, and the God we've grown to love seems distant.

One of the primary reasons I've been drawn to this story in recent years is because of what Jesus accomplished by walking on the water. It's not the miracle of simply doing the impossible. It's that Jesus stood on top of a storm. It's that he walked on and—more importantly—over and through the waves. In the challenges that we experience, we feel the rock of the boat, yet we sense that Jesus must be near.

What Binghampton Teaches Us about Faith

We live in Binghampton, which is in an urban community in Memphis. Some would say that it is an underprivileged and under-resourced community. Our experiences confirm that it is a community rich in culture and opportunity.

One of our disciplines to make sure we are connecting with neighbors is to spend time outside playing ball, sitting in chairs enjoying the breeze, or chasing our dog. I had no clue how much our little Westie dog (named Grizz, after the Memphis NBA team) would open doors for conversation. Another reason dogs are better than cats. Dogs are a magnet for neighbors.

We live in a neighborhood with a lot of foot traffic, and being outside gives us a chance to interact with friends. Recently, a young girl, probably eleven or twelve years old, walked by our home. We had never met this girl before, though we have gotten to know her since this first encounter. She stopped at our home, and the first thing she said to us was, "Y'all are from Texas, aren't you?"

You see, Kayci and I loved growing up in Texas, but neither of us has bought into the Texas ego that everything under the sun is bigger and better in Texas (except for high school football, of course!). We don't have Texas bumper stickers. We don't wave Texas flags. And other than Mavericks and Cowboys T-shirts, we don't wear Texas paraphernalia. So we weren't sure why she thought we were from Texas.

"Y'all are from Texas, aren't you?"

"Well, actually we are, but how did you know that?"

Without hesitating, she responded, "All white people are from Texas."

Let's be honest. We all know Texans who think that everything is from Texas, and I'm sure there are those who do think that white people came from Texas.

We responded, "Some are. But not all of us are. In fact, some white people were born right here in Memphis."

"Really???"

"Sure. Where are you from?"

"I'm from right here in Binghampton."

"Well, Binghampton is a great place to be from."

Her quick response cut to the heart.

"No, it ain't. We get shot and we die around here."

How would you have responded to this young girl whose life experiences had shaped her worldview to respond in such a way?

All we could think to say was something like this: "How about we try to love in a way that we change that?"

When we choose to believe that the people in our cities are worth fighting and living for, then we are called into deeper forms of engagement. Yet here's the kicker: when we engage our local contexts, we find ourselves wading into deep water. Waves keep coming. Cultural waves. Systematic waves. Societal waves. Waves induced by sin. Waves induced by circumstances. Waves induced by neglect, abuse, apathy, and fear.

Jesus could have yelled at his followers in the boat, "Stay there! I'm coming to you! Don't come to me . . . it's too dangerous out here. I'll come to you. Stay safe in the boat. Here I come."

Count on Jesus to do the unexpected.

Peter said, "Lord, if it's you, tell me to come." Peter is the one who asked for permission.

Jesus: "Come on."

We don't have Peter's verbal response, but I wonder if he looked at his buddies and said, "Did he really just say to come on? I didn't really mean it. Seriously, I was just joking. You all knew I was joking, right?"

It's Peter's move next. What do you do? Leave the safety of the boat to venture out into the waves? Or play it safe and trust that Jesus will make his way to you?

There are too many Christians and too many churches who have become masters at playing it safe in the boat, and we do it under the names of holiness, sanctification, and keeping ourselves from being polluted by the world. I've seen way too many people choose the comfort of a Sunday morning worship hour over the mission of a church time and time again. Yet, we fail to see that in the Bible, holiness was not used as an excuse to separate from the world but as empowerment by God to faithfully engage the world.

The waves of life seem high, and often it is because they are, yet the voice of Jesus can still be heard in the waves. "I'm here in the thick of the chaos. Will you come and join me? Walk. Move. Jump in. Because there is a God to serve. There are people in the waves to love. Let's go!"

∽

In Barrow, storms come in the forms of snow, ice, high winds, and blistering cold. But there are emotional, social, and psychological storms that come in the forms of isolation, loneliness, despair, and abuse.

One night while I was in Barrow, I had dinner with one of their police officers. He was gracious to let me ask him a lot of questions about crime. Some of his responses surprised me. For example, they don't have to worry about car theft in Barrow. The only way to get in and out of Barrow is either by ship or plane. There are no roads leading out of the city. And people don't have garages. So, there is nowhere to drive a stolen vehicle.

He told me that many of the calls he has to respond to are for domestic abuse. In Memphis, it's the number-one reason police roll their wheels; the same is true for Barrow. There are smaller homes and large families. And for those families with dads who drink a lot in the winter, it can make for a bad combination. The stories he shared of abuse were horrifying.

The people I talked with in Barrow shared that the best thing people can do when the temperatures are well below freezing is to make yourself get out of the home. Go to the store. Go to the library. Go to a high school basketball game. Don't settle. Just get up. And walk!

Walking when we don't want to is one of the hardest things to do in life, yet it can also be the very thing that brings us health, joy, and maturity.

Walking in the Storm

Walking is the exact thing Jesus and Peter did together. But something else happened first.

"But when he [Peter] noticed the strong wind, he became frightened, and beginning to sink, he cried out, 'Lord, save me!'" (Matt. 14:30).

Who would blame him, right? At least Peter gave it a shot. It's not like he had much practice walking on water.

Don't let Peter's stumble keep you from seeing what happens next.

"Jesus immediately reached out his hand and caught him" (v. 31).

Jesus caught him.

He didn't just help Peter up.

He caught him.

This isn't the image of someone drowning, and a friend lifts them up.

This is the image of someone falling, and the one beside him catching him before he hits the surface.

Then, all we are told is this, "When they got into the boat . . ."

Come on, Matthew! Give us some more details, bro. That's it? How? How did they get back into the boat? How far did they walk? Did Jesus pull some hocus-pocus trick and they magically were teleported from the water into the boat?

We aren't given the details, but if you stop to think about it, Jesus and Peter walked together, despite the wind and waves, back to the boat.

They walked together.

Over the waves.

The wind didn't cease until they got back to the boat. Jesus could have calmed the waves to make the walk easier, but he didn't.

"When they got into the boat, the wind ceased. And those in the boat worshiped him, saying, 'Truly you are the Son of God'" (Matt. 14:32–33).

They worshipped the One who walked through and over the storms. Did you know this is the only time the word *worship* is used in Matthew, Mark, and Luke to describe an act that is giving glory and affection to Jesus? We have people worshipping Jesus at his birth and after the resurrection, but this is the only time we have a worship service with the word *worship* used. And it is when Jesus conquers the storm.

Jesus didn't only want Peter to know that he is there to catch him when he falls, but that he invites his adventurous followers to venture out into the winds, storms, and waves, and that together with Jesus, we victoriously walk over them!

Storms Don't Define Us

At Sycamore View, we launched a Celebrate Recovery (CR) ministry a few years ago. A few times a year, I get to hang out with them. And every single time I do, I get a piece of heaven.

CR was born in the early 1990s as a recovery program focused on hurts, habits, and hang-ups. Its founders, John Baker and Rick

Warren, were looking for a program that was more Christ-focused than Alcoholics Anonymous, as well as something that was broader. CR includes alcohol and drug addiction, but it also has members struggling with bankruptcy, codependency, anger, etc.

Anyone who plays a leadership role during a CR worship setting stands in front of the group and says something like, "Hi, my name is _____. I am a grateful believer in Jesus Christ, and I struggle with _____." First is your name and identity, and then your struggle.

In other words, first is what God says you are, and second is what God is working to deliver you from.

Said another way, your identity in Jesus comes before the unhealthy waves of life. The storms don't define us, though they sure will try. Salvation comes with a brand-new identity.

Faithfully Remembering the Storms

Peter needed this moment, because it strengthened his faith in Jesus. It taught him about trust, risk, and what it means to be victorious.

For the rest of Peter's life, I think that moment on the lake is one he remembered often. Through prison sentences, near-death experiences, persecution, and standing before religious rulers, Peter remembered that the One who called him out of the boat was also the One who walked with him over the storms of life.

Whether it's a disciple who needed to take a risk, the death of a loved one, or anything else, Jesus teaches us that no matter how our circumstances attempt to permanently define us, the call of God is inviting us—and sometimes reinviting us—into his heart and mission. His ways are worth living for, dying for, and fighting for.

Note
[1] Josh Graves and Chris Seidman, *Heaven on Earth: Realizing the Good Life Now* (Nashville: Abingdon Press, 2012), 26, 29.

CHAPTER 5

Jesus on Repeat

It has been over seven years since my sister, Jenny, passed away. Yet I still remember certain images, smells, and sounds from that hospital in Fort Worth as if it was yesterday.

I remember the sound of over a hundred people filling a waiting room with encouragement, support, and prayer.

I remember places where my mother would hide from people to let out a good cry.

I remember watching Super Bowl XLIV on a small television in a quiet waiting room, and not caring who won.

I remember friends bringing me energy drinks, Chick-fil-A breakfast, and numerous changes of clothes.

I also vividly remember the long hallway that became the scene for a story that has been shared in books, on stages, and in numerous other settings.

After an excruciating eighteen-day fight, Jenny breathed her last breath the afternoon of February 22, while a faithful doctor stood singing *It Is Well* over her dying body:

"It is well, it is well with my soul!"

I wasn't there to see my parents walk out of the hospital that February afternoon. But we've talked about it so many times, I feel like I can visualize it all.

My mom stopped my dad, because there was a question she had to ask before they ventured into the parking lot.

Actually, I'm not sure why my mom stopped to ask the question. I'm sure there was a part of her that didn't want to face the reality of her oldest child not making it past the age of thirty-one. I'd imagine there was the nauseating ache of knowing they had to get in a car with my brother-in-law and drive to a home to tell their nine-year-old granddaughter the news no parent or grandparent ever wants to have to relay.

In that hallway, my mom wanted to grab my dad's shirt in anxiety, but she simply placed her hands on his chest.

"Rick, before we walk out of here, remind me what it is we believe. What is it that we know to be true?"

And the four words flowed from my dad that have become a rallying cry for the brokenhearted: "The tomb is empty!"

You know what is difficult? It is when we know that the road moving forward is going to look very little like the road we have left behind.

It is when the loved one who has passed isn't coming back.

It is when the job position has been eliminated, and a new way forward is the only option.

It is when aggressive cancer hits, and the impact is felt by the entire family and close sphere of influence.

It's when a sin has led someone down a destructive path, and it has harmed dozens along the way. After all, there is no such thing as a secret sin that doesn't have a major impact on everyone else.

It's not that God can't redeem a person, but that his redemption doesn't erase the past. The blood of Jesus doesn't function like the flashy thing from *Men in Black* that has the power to wipe the past from your memory. Instead, it reframes the past so it can be viewed through what Jesus has accomplished in death, burial, and resurrection.

The presence of God is the constant. It is the very thing that transcends the past, present, and future. Yet the presence of God doesn't mean that navigating through shifts, turns, and transitions in life won't be difficult.

∿

The Barrow school counselor struck a chord when he said that he begins to feel symptoms of depression when the sun returns, because he expects that the light will bring change. However, it doesn't.

Instead, as the sun returns, the elements remain. The weather remains the same. The ice won't go away.

What happens in life when we experience a breakthrough, yet the elements remain?

Fresh starts aren't void of numerous memories and present-day reminders of the past.

The greatest growth, maturity, and spiritual development often come when we press through the pain of confusing, difficult, challenging transitions and shifts in life. Yet, too many times, we get two feet into the transitional waves and we quit because of the discomfort and uncertainty that await us in the future.

When we have been dealt cards in life that we would rather not have in our hand, what do we do?

When we're initiated into clubs we never wanted to be in (widowhood, divorced, bankruptcy, moral failure, etc.), how do we find our way again?

Back in Boats

So far, we have seen Peter get into a boat twice, and leave a boat for Jesus twice. He left a boat to enter into a life of discipleship.

He left a boat to walk on the storm. It was about radical trust, risk, surrender, and adventure.

Let me introduce (or reintroduce) you to one more. I'm not saying this one is more important than Luke 5 or Matthew 14, but for the sake of this book, getting our minds and hearts around John 21 will propel us for the rest of our journey together.

It's the last chapter in what we call "the Gospels." This was after Jesus had been raised from the dead, and we read, "They went out and got into the boat" (John 21:3).

Why were they back in the boat? It's kind of ambiguous, isn't it? Sometimes the Bible does this to us. It doesn't paint stories with every detail, emotion, and intention of the heart. It drives some people crazy, but I really don't mind. It allows us to be curious, to ask questions, and to think through what it would have been like to be there.

Were they back in a boat because they had returned to their former lives as fishermen? They could do this without giving up on Jesus. They could have acknowledged how great Jesus was, yet return to the boats because they didn't have anything else to live for anymore. Or maybe Peter reached a point where he no longer thought he could be used by Jesus.

What we know about boats in the Bible is that many times boats create distance between people and God, people and a mission, or people and people. Similarly, boats are often obstacles to overcome.

Boats were about safety, security, occupation, therapy, and transportation, and isn't that the problem in John 21? These fishermen had left their jobs for Jesus three and a half years earlier, and now that Jesus had died, they were back in the boats. Maybe they were back in the boats because it was their safe place; like a hobby that clears the mind and brings some peace. But maybe it was because they had decided to go back to their former lives.

Following Jesus had been adventurous, but things hadn't gone as planned. It was fun while it lasted, but now it was back to reality.

How do we get back in the boats today?

How often do we settle for the average, instead of pressing into what is better?

Why do we become companions with mediocrity, instead of engaging hope as the only thing that matters?

In the Western world, I see people opt for safety and comfort more than faith and risk because our culture—even our church culture—has taught us to do just that. "I chose this church because it made me feel the most comfortable," is not a phrase you find in the Bible. Far from it! I see people choose churches based on comfort and familiarity over mission and vision way too often. I fear it is because we have been duped into thinking that the call of the church is to protect the establishment more than to restore the world.

We often confuse being safe in the boat with being safe in the arms of God, but it's not always this way. We can trick ourselves into thinking that God is only in the calm waters, yet sometimes God is in the waves, on the waves, and the One who created the waves.

Peter and his friends were in a boat again, and the fish still weren't biting. I'm not questioning Peter's fishing ability, but both times we have him fishing in the Bible, he can't even get a nibble. However, what makes him as a fisherman different from my grandpa is that Peter stayed out all night trying. If Papa didn't have a bite in the first fifteen seconds, he called it quits.

They were about a hundred yards from shore when a voice shouted for them to cast their nets on the other side of the boat. It was Jesus, but they didn't know it. There was distance between them. They obeyed the voice and caught a netful, but what is interesting—unlike Luke 5—is that this time the nets didn't break and the boat didn't sink.

I'll let you ask Peter one day about John 21:7: "When Simon Peter heard that it was the Lord, he put on some clothes, for he was naked, and jumped into the sea." We'll assume that either he was hot, or he was working on his tan for the next vacation with his wife. Either way, he put on clothes to jump in the sea, and then channeled his inner Michael Phelps by swimming a hundred yards. I'm sure he alternated between breaststroke, butterfly, tread-water-take-a-breath, breaststroke, freestyle, etc.

Peter was faced with a decision: *Stay in the boat or jump out of the boat?*

There was distance and an obstacle between him and Jesus, and he decided to immediately do something that would shrink the distance. And he went for it.

Take a moment to read all of John 21. Seriously. It's a fascinating chapter. Yet, here's what I want to focus on for a few moments . . . the very last phrase Jesus uses in John's Gospel is this: *Follow me!* If you have a red-letter edition, you can see it. It's the phrase Jesus invites people into relationship with, and it is the phrase that keeps being repeated. *"Follow me"* is invitation and entrance into a vibrant relationship with God, and it is also the phrase that continually comes from heaven, inviting us into deeper places with God and his mission. It is the phrase that keeps on coming.

The boat was once Peter's life, but now Jesus was his life.

The boat was once his place of security, but now Jesus was.

The boat was once his source of income, but now Jesus changed how he thought about spending.

Jesus called Peter into discipleship, into salvation, but he didn't stop calling him. He kept speaking, inviting, affirming, and commissioning.

And what Jesus did for Peter, he does for you too.

John 21 is not about entry into covenant or salvation. John 21 is about reentry into mission and joyful adventure. John 21 is about reengagement.

I don't know what you are most in need of right now. It may be entry into a relationship with Jesus like in Luke 5. Maybe your life feels like you are being tossed by the waves, and you are in need of deeper trust like in Matthew 14. Or maybe you are in need of reengaging the heart and mission of Jesus because you have been through a season that has been confusing, difficult, frustrating, disappointing, and downright chaotic.

I'm with people every week who often express how they feel too broken, too hurt, too bitter, too lonely, or too sinful to be used by God. Part of that is that the church hasn't always taught and modeled the grace of God as faithfully as we should have.

Yet, part of it is that Satan and all of his friends are eager to convince us that we aren't good enough, or that the mistakes we have made have disqualified us as instruments in the hands of God to be used for good.

Damaged Beauty

A while back I came across a form of Japanese art called *kintsugi*. Apparently it is priceless, in that it produces what are considered magnificent works of art. It is broken pieces of pottery that have been put back together again.

Barbara Bloom describes it like this, "When the Japanese mend broken objects, they aggrandize the damage by filling the cracks with gold. They believe that when something has suffered damage and has a history it becomes more beautiful."

Damaged beauty. Can there be such a thing?

Jesus says, "Absolutely!"

We turn to Jesus for salvation, yet we turn to television, food, technology, and forms of medication for comfort, pleasure, and satisfaction.

We trust in our homes, beds, recliners, and clothes to bring comfort and identity, and yet wonder why weariness persists.

Some have argued that John doesn't belong in the Bible between Luke and Acts, because Luke wrote both Luke and Acts. However, I think John 21 belongs right before Acts.

Without John 21, and how Jesus modeled reentry and reengagement, the disciples would have been hesitant the rest of their lives, not brave.

The Gospels end with reentry. The Gospels end as the Gospels began—calling the nobodies to change the world.

Without John 21, some of the events in Acts wouldn't have happened. The disciples would have been walking on eggshells. They would have been overly cautious. They would have been afraid of failure. But instead, you have these people who caught hold of the fire of God, and they breathed it in, and lived it out.

The "Follow me" from Jesus keeps coming!

Do you ever feel like there are days when the powers of darkness and evil aren't just winning, but they're running up the score while they do it? I do.

Moments when you can be discouraged are numerous! There is ISIS, Ferguson, Baltimore, Charlotte, the immigration crisis, cops who were shot in Dallas, hurricanes that have devastated places like Haiti, domestic abuse, a heated and toxic presidential election season . . . and the list just keeps going.

Yet, when it seems like there is more discouragement to grab on to than hope, don't be fooled. Latch on to hope. Cling to it.

Getting Better and Following

We sometimes get into boats to find temporary relief from the pains of life, but God has something better to offer us.

But, like Peter, are we willing to swim the hundred yards to get to the presence of Jesus?

It's not that God's attitude is that he'll meet us halfway if we'll go halfway. God is too merciful, gracious, and good to play those kinds of games.

But you know what? I think God does want us to show how committed we are to experience healing, restoration, redemption, and reentry.

I've seen too many people who want Jesus as their healer, but persist in living as if they are in a permanent state of needing to be in ICU for the rest of their lives. No one was meant to stay in ICU forever. The goal of ICU is to get you better so you can go thrive in life as a healthier person.

One thing that really frustrates me is when I meet with a husband and wife who are going through a dark time. There may be some serious dysfunction in their marriage. I point them to a therapist so they can receive long-term care. But then they inform me that they don't want to go because it is too expensive. I'm like, "You have got to be kidding me right now! You are willing to spend ten thousand dollars on a wedding, yet you aren't willing to spend a thousand dollars over a few months to repair your marriage?"

Here's the deal. I don't want people—I don't want you—to settle for mediocrity, when Jesus is inviting you into something so much better!

"*Follow me*" is what Jesus said. This is more than thinking as he thinks. It is to live as he lived. It is to get dressed. Put on your shoes. Brush your teeth. Stand up on your feet. And get moving! There's a mission to engage in, and God has invited you into it.

To Peter, it's as if Jesus said, "Blessed are you, because even though you denied and betrayed me, I want nothing more than to set your heart on fire for the mission God has for you."

And what God did for Peter, he wants to do for all of us too.

Get out of the boat, because Jesus is serving up a feast.

And you are invited.

PART 2

Roots

Kayci and I met our freshman year of college, began dating our sophomore year, got engaged our junior year, and got married right before our senior year. However, unfortunately, we can't remember when we met. It's awful. We want that story that you find in a book by Nicholas Sparks or in a Valentine's Day movie. We've debated making one up just so we have a story to share.

We came into college with a thousand other eighteen- to nineteen-year-olds, and we ran in similar groups. We think it may have been in a small group setting at church one Sunday morning that we met.

By our sophomore year, we began dating. Well, kind of. It wasn't that easy. Better said, I pursued, she ran. And this went on for a few months. Kayci went to college after having come out of a high school relationship that was both verbally and emotionally abusive. She wasn't looking for a serious relationship. I had dated quite a bit in high school and my freshman year of college, but I knew that I was ready to settle down with the next relationship. So, come our sophomore year, we liked each other, but our expectations were polar opposites.

Strangely enough, we ended up in astronomy together during the fall of our sophomore year. It's like it was meant to be. We went to class to learn about the stars. And we sat on the back row while learning . . . or while attempting to learn. Midway through the semester, I had done my homework. I'm not referring to astronomy homework, but "how-to-date-Kayci" homework.

I considered using some Will Smith pickup lines from *Fresh Prince of Bel-Air*. Things like, "Girl, I wish I could plant you and grow a field of y'all." Or, "Girl, your feet must be tired because you've been running through my mind all day." They seemed to work so well for him. So, why not, right?

Instead, I paid attention to things she liked. I found out she had a deep love for Snickers candy. So I would come into every class with a Snickers for her. I discovered she liked yellow roses with pink tips. Every other week, I would walk into class with one. I was told she thought it was hot when guys wore their hats backward. So, even if I had a suit and tie on (I was pledging), I would still have a hat on backward.

After a few months of chasing, we began dating. And the rest is history.

One thing that was quite ironic is that the first movie we watched together was *The Preacher's Wife*, starring Denzel Washington and Whitney Houston. It was toward the end of the movie that it hit us this could become our reality.

The night I proposed to her, I took her to a lake where I wrote her a song and where we had our first dance. The song I wrote her was called "You Are My Princess." It had four verses and a chorus. I've never been known for singing very well, and after singing her the first two verses, she put her hand on my shoulder and said, "This is beautiful. It means the world to me, but can you just speak the last two verses?" Our first dance was awkward, and not because we can't dance, but because the only CD I had in my truck at the time was by Third Day. Our first dance in the headlights was to *Who Is This King of Glory*? Thanks, Mac Powell!

I went back to that lake to propose, and I used the cover of the *Preacher's Wife* VHS tape to do it. I placed a picture of Kayci over Whitney Houston, and a picture of me over Denzel Washington. When I got on a knee, I had the VHS cover and the ring on top of it. Pretty romantic, huh?

Kayci and I were blessed with parents who modeled healthy marriages for us. Being in the Abilene environment for a few years also provided us with multiple marriage mentor couples. Thankfully, we didn't enter marriage attempting to break cycles of witnessing abusive patterns. Yet, as we went through premarital counseling, read books, and attempted marriage seminars in preparation for our own marriage, we had to take time to discern what our marriage was going to be founded on. What was going to be the foundation of our family? What were the three to five concrete convictions and principles that would serve as our launching points moving forward, and measuring sticks reflecting backward?

A lesson the Lord has pressed into me over the past few years is that marriage is not about two people growing in love for the rest of their lives. It is about two people learning to love one another, while also realizing that their marriage is not for them alone, but that it becomes a witness to the world of the faithfulness of God. God's design for marriage is that it is an extension of his mercy. It's an expression of his covenant.

What are we going to build this on?

It's a great question to ask for a marriage, and it's a great question to ask in life.

What are the principles that are unshakable? What are the values that are immovable?

Where are our roots going to be established?

What happens when tragedy hits, the bank account runs low, kids enter the picture, the job is demanding, and life is hard?

What do we fall back on? How have we allowed roots to grow, spread, and run deep? Without established roots, fruit dries up, leaves wither, and the flowers fade. With established roots, the weather may change and elements may become harsh, but the heart is able to live from a place of purpose, joy, hope, and meaning, because it is rooted in something (or someone) of substance.

While in Barrow, as I sat with people asking them what principles help them through the harsh elements, darkness, and the freezing cold, two words kept coming up. It wasn't a mantra in that these two words hung on billboards or were a part of their school fight song. But people spoke of them as if the two words had been woven into the fabric of their communal lives.

Roots.

Rhythm.

Roots and *rhythm.*

With them, the heart of a person or a community remains strong. Without them, people can forget who they are, why they are, where they are, and what they are.

Forests Exist Because of Roots

I'm a huge fan of the Bay Area. It's one of my favorite places to visit in the United States. I used to joke with Kayci that we should plant a church in that area, but unfortunately, my southern accent would definitely keep me from being very effective. It would be too much of a distraction.

I first visited San Francisco on a spring break campaign my freshman year of college. It was one of the milestone weeks of my life with Jesus. It was then that God opened me up to the marginalized, the poor, the oppressed, the broken, and the hurting like never before. God taught me that week that homeless people have names, that inmates in the city jail are redeemable, that drug addicts can be made whole again, and that gays and lesbians on Castro Street are human beings created in the image of God just like everyone else.

One afternoon, our group leaders took us to Muir Woods. It's a forest full of redwood trees. We huddled up, and our leaders encouraged each of us to take one hour to find somewhere to honor some time with the Lord in silence, prayer, and meditation.

I found a spot over a running stream. I sat there on a tiny bridge. I encountered God there in some profound ways. As only God can, he reminded me both of his unfailing love and of sin that I had allowed to settle into my heart. Before leaving that place, I took a moment to journal about the experience.

Years later, when Kayci and I took a trip to the Bay Area, we went back to Muir Woods, and I took her to that place. It has been a pillar on my spiritual walk. A moment of deep conviction. A place of God's mysterious presence that meets us when we are open to his activity and intervention.

Muir Woods is like a sanctuary. It is peaceful, quiet, and spectacular. The massive redwood trees reach to the heavens, forming a canopy. You can't help but stand in awe at the trees, which grow to heights of over three hundred feet. You almost feel like you must whisper while standing next to your friend, as if you have approached the altar of God.

You would think that trees that grow taller than the length of a football field and wide enough to drive your car through would have roots reaching deep into the ground, forming death grips in order to keep the tree healthy, growing, and safe. Yet, that's not the case. The roots of a redwood are quite shallow, usually measuring only five or six feet deep; but what they lack in depth, they make up in width. The roots often extend over a hundred feet from the trunk, and they entangle themselves with the roots of other redwoods, forming bonds that allow for growth and great strength. Redwoods don't grow by themselves. They grow in groups.

Scientists and researchers estimate that hundreds of gallons of water flow through the redwoods each day. This is why they thrive in river bottoms. For water to flow to the top of a tree, it takes strong, healthy, vibrant roots. It takes a heart the size of a basketball to pump blood to the head of a giraffe, and it takes healthy roots to pump water to the top of a redwood.

As you tour Muir Woods, occasionally you'll see roots sticking out of the ground; but for the most part, they go unnoticed; maybe even unappreciated. Yet the health of the tree, and the forest sanctuary, is totally dependent on what happens underneath.

The redwood forest has a lot to teach kingdom people.

How and where are roots being cultivated?

How close are we allowing ourselves to grow in community?

What gives us strength to endure the storms from above is dependent on how we allow our roots to grow beneath.

Roots and *rhythm*.

Before flipping to the next chapter, take a moment to let this sink in from Ephesians 3:16–19:

> I pray that, according to the riches of his glory, he may grant that you may be strengthened in your inner being with power through his Spirit, and that Christ may dwell in your hearts through faith, as you are being rooted and grounded in love. I pray that you may have the power to comprehend, with all the saints, what is the breadth and length and height and depth, and to know the love of Christ that surpasses knowledge, so that you may be filled with all the fullness of God.

CHAPTER 6

Establishing Roots

I grew up in Dallas exactly thirty miles from Six Flags Over Texas. Thirty miles could mean thirty minutes or two hours, depending on the time of day and road construction. Every summer, our youth group participated in Soul Lift, a two-day event where we would meet on a Sunday night with dozens of other churches for an evening of worship and encouragement, and then on Monday, we would all go to Six Flags. The day would end with a concert at the amphitheater in the amusement park.

This was back in the 1990s, so a day at Six Flags meant blue jean shorts, cutoff shirts, white socks, and tennis shoes, with fanny packs for the adult volunteers. Or another way to think of it is that Six Flags, in Dallas, in the summer, is like visiting an amusement park on the surface of the sun. By the time you got to the evening concert, no one wanted to lift his or her hands in worship or in applause, because deodorant quit working around 2:00 P.M. when you got drenched on the Splash Water Falls to cool off.

One year, three of us decided to do the only ride you have to pay for once you have already paid to get into the park: the Dive Bomber. For $18 a person, they would strap you onto the thrill of all thrills. Lying parallel to the ground, you are lifted up to around

220 feet, and then after a free fall of 125 feet, you swing on a bungee cord until you come to a stop.

I was in the middle, a guy friend was on my left, and a girl friend of ours was on the right. As they began to lift us in the air, the girl to my right began crying . . . hysterically! I don't remember a tear; I remember one of those shoulder-bouncing, snot-dripping cries. She wanted down. But once on, the only way you come off the Dive Bomber is to ride the Dive Bomber. I'm sure the employees working the ride love those moments when people begin to cry as soon as they start to ascend. They smile, wave, and blame it on corporate. "They won't let us stop the ride, for safety reasons. You'll be fine. Just close your eyes. It'll be over shortly."

Knowing we still had over two hundred feet to climb, I asked her if there was anything I could do for her. Did she want me to tell her a joke? Sing a song? Lead a prayer? I was willing to do all three if it would help. Through her sobs, she said, "I want you to sing me a song."

Have you ever been in a moment and a song comes to you that fits the moment you're in? Well, that's exactly what happened to me. The first song that came to me was a song we used to sing in the youth group, "Lord, be there for me when I fall . . . be there for me when I fall . . . be there for me, dear Lord."

Needless to say, the song didn't go over well. After elbowing me in the ribs, she actually had the audacity to say, "Sing me another song."

The next song that came to mind wasn't any better. It was an ancient hymn, "Some glad morning when this life is o'er, I'll fly away, fly away. To a home on God's celestial shore, I'll fly away, fly away."

Another elbow in the ribs.

By that time, we were close to the top. As we hovered in the air, it was time to pull the cord. As we began our free fall, she screamed as a girl, and I screamed like a girl. I was kind of embarrassed that a fierce scream of that magnitude came out of this body. In fact, after the ride, friends came up and asked if that high-pitched shrill came out of me. With a low voice, I was adamant that it did not.

The Roller Coasters of Life

I'm not sure if roller coasters and bungee cords are your thing or not. They aren't for everyone. Some rides have height, weight, health, and age requirements. At amusement parks, roller coasters are optional. It is your choice. People may beg you to join them on a ride, but no one forces you to ride. You pay the money, enter the park, and make choices to ride or abstain.

However, the roller coaster of life isn't optional. In life, it often seems like roller coasters choose us more than we choose them. Events happen in life, and next thing you know, it feels like you are being taken on a ride, and you have little to no control. It sometimes feels like you're on a ride and there is no way off, no end in sight, and the only things in front of you are more obstacles, loops, and screaming people.

David Was in for a Ride

When the prophet Samuel anointed David as the future king of Israel, David had no clue the journey he would have to take to get there. If he had known, I wonder if he would have refused the anointing. It wasn't going to be a peaceful transition of power. It was going to be quite a ride.

Immediately after David was anointed king in 1 Samuel 16, he began to play the harp for Saul whenever an evil spirit came upon him. Not bad, right? Your first assignment was to use your gift in a way that made the powers of darkness flee. A boost in confidence? Check.

Then, you have that whole chapter about Goliath. It's one of the most well-known stories in the Bible. It's the go-to story of the Old Testament. What I mean by that is when the teacher for a Sunday children's class calls in sick, this is the go-to story. It never disappoints. The underdog wins. The giant falls. Another event affirming that Samuel got the anointing right? Check.

After Goliath, David had a best friend for life (Jonathan), and King Saul gave him more and more power and authority. Saul promoted him to head of the army. A few months back he was a shepherd watching over his dad's sheep, and now he found himself leading the greatest army in the world. Not bad.

Up to that point, everything seemed to be going as planned. There was success, promotion, advancement, and divine favor.

Everything changed when the cheerleaders stepped onto the scene. There weren't just a few of them. There were lots of them. A little chant turned the tide.

Saul has killed his thousands,
And David his ten thousands.

The people chanted what was reality. However, Saul didn't like where this story was heading. And David's life was about to become chaotic, confusing, and stressful.

On two different occasions, Saul threw a spear at David in an attempt to pin him against a wall. Twice!!! Do you know how many times I would let someone miss while throwing a spear at me? Once. I would take off running and never return. I would change my address. Take on a fake name. Grow out my beard. Wear shades. And walk with my head down. That person would never get a chance to throw another spear at me again.

Not David. He trusted in the plan.

Saul promised David one of his daughters as a wife; yet when it came time, she was given to someone else.

Later, David was promised another of the king's daughters if he could present Saul with one hundred Philistine foreskins. What happened to bride prices with cattle, lambs, and a little cash? Saul wanted David to die in the fight (1 Sam. 18:25). But David did it. He won a wife.

Then David's life became a life on the run. He lost his friends. His home became a cave. In fact, by the end of 1 Samuel 21, David couldn't take it anymore, or so it seemed. So, he went into the land of his enemies, and he got to the point that he pretended to be someone he was not. Then we are told this:

> David took these words to heart and was very much afraid of King Achish of Gath. So he changed his behavior before them; he pretended to be mad when in their presence. He scratched marks on the doors of the gate, and let his spittle run down his beard. (1 Sam. 21:12–13)

When we find ourselves caught up in the roller coaster of life, it is easy for us to lose our footing on our foundation. We forget our story. We neglect our roots. And if we're not careful, we slowly become someone we are not. It can happen to the best of us. After all, it happened to the one the Bible calls "a man after God's own heart."

Unexpected Waves

Kayci and I take a trip every year with no kids. It's a commitment we have honored since we had our first child, Truitt, in 2007. For us, it is important to get away and to enjoy each other with as few distractions as possible. So, once a year, we toss our kids to my parents, and we go. We have taken a few cruises, gone to an occasional all-inclusive resort, or traveled and stayed downtown in some of our favorite cities like San Francisco, Boston, or Chicago.

In 2015, we traveled to Cabo for a few days. We had never been, so we decided to give it a shot. We saved our big excursion for the final night. So, after a few days of great food and needed relaxation, we jumped on the shuttle toward our grand adventure.

When people heard we were going to Cabo, we were told we had to take a dinner cruise to see the arch. It's a three-deck dinner cruise, and for two hours, you go out to sea, dance to music, eat fajitas, and enjoy the scenery. Unfortunately, we failed to watch the weather channel before we went. But who watches the weather channel on vacation? We were in Cabo. The weather hardly ever changes. We had no clue a tropical storm was coming in the next day.

As we left the port, we began to feel the waves, and as we rounded the corner into the bay, we no longer just felt them, we could see them. We were going over twelve-foot waves, and they wouldn't stop. One after another. Up. Down. Up. Down.

My phobia in life is vomit. I hate everything about it. Now, I'm not one of those people who puke if I see other people puke. Instead, I just despise pukers for a few months . . . or years. I will spare you the details, but on that dinner cruise, people were losing it everywhere; in bathrooms, stairwells, overboard, on the deck. It was my hell on earth.

Kayci and I sat down with our backs up against a wall. And we stayed there. We closed our eyes, held hands, breathed deeply, and prayed for Jesus to come back. At one point, I almost prayed one of those prayers: "God, if you deliver me from this, and keep me from getting sick, I will give half of what I have to the poor. I will never look down on New York Yankees fans again. I will do anything. Just get me off this boat."

One of the employees began walking around offering free shots of tequila. I'm not a big tequila guy, but I almost asked for the entire tray. Anything to just knock me out.

Thankfully, we made it back to shore and got off the boat without losing our stomachs, or our minds. We hugged each other, the ground, and even complete strangers. We were alive!

Reflecting back on that night, we discussed the feeling of complete helplessness. When you're on a boat in a storm, there is nothing you can do. Nothing. You're just stuck. And the waves keep coming. They won't stop. They only multiply.

I spend a lot of my time with people who are living life on waves like we experienced in Cabo. Some are on the turbulent waves because of poor decisions; others, because of decisions made by those they love; and others because life sometimes throws curveballs that we were never expecting.

From the Mouths of Children

Kayci and I want to teach our boys to cry out to God for themselves and others. In our attempts to teach them to intercede for others, we give them a lot of responsibility in our prayer time, and we encourage them to pray with authority. And when my boys pray, you never know what you're going to get.

The other night at dinner, here was one of their prayers:

Dear God,

I wonder if Satan likes football. Because sometimes I think Satan thinks he is winning. But Satan is on his own one-yard line. He thinks he's good. But then you sack him for a safety, which means you get two points, and you also get the ball. Then, you score on him. Then, you score again . . . and again . . . and again. And you keep doing that until you usher in the new heaven and the new earth.

In Jesus's name, amen!

Football and theology. I wish I could say he gets that from his mom.

In the summer of 2016, we lost a young man in our church. His name was Tamarie. He was only twenty-one when he passed.

In the August heat, he suffered a heat stroke and his body couldn't recover. It was tragic for our church family, and for all of Tamarie's sphere of influence.

The night before he passed away, my boys asked to intercede in prayer over Tamarie. There are days when my boys rush through a prayer so they can eat their Chick-fil-A nuggets, or get back to their toys, and then there are days when they pray from a deep place I'm unable to teach. It's like the Spirit of God is simply breathing life through them. It was one of those nights.

> *Dear God,*
>
> *Sometimes it feels like Satan jumps on our back and won't let us go. And when he jumps on our back, he wants to inject us with poison from our head to our toes. And when he is on our back, it's like we can't get him off. We can't shake him.*

(In that moment, my son began to act this out in his prayer time. He wasn't being funny. It was like he was talking to God about the inability to shake evil and darkness sometimes.)

> *And God, that's what Satan is doing to Tamarie right now. He jumped on his back and he won't get off. But God, remind Satan tonight, that just when he thought he was going to win, Jesus jumped on his back, and Jesus destroyed him forever. Please, God, do that for Tamarie.*
>
> *In Jesus's name, amen!*

Have you ever felt like the enemy jumped on your back and won't get off? Maybe you're in one of those seasons where you feel like you just can't shake him off. It's like he has a death grip.

Where are our roots? What is our core? What do we fall back on?

In Times of Testing, Where Do You Run?

Back to David.

Things weren't going well for him. After being anointed by Samuel, defeating a giant, and progressing in favor with God and others, his life took a turn for the worse. He was hunted by a king, betrayed by friends, and his permanent address was either in caves or in the land of the enemies. This isn't how he imagined his life playing out.

There's a verse tucked away in the middle of all this chaos. In fact, it is tucked away so well that some of you have read it, but you didn't even notice it. In the middle of chaos, distress, doubt, and confusion, we get this:

"Now David fled and escaped; he came to Samuel at Ramah, and told him all that Saul had done to him" (1 Sam. 19:18).

I read that, and I want to know more.

In the middle of enormous unrest, David went back to the place of his anointing. He went back to Samuel. It's the first encounter we have between the two since Samuel anointed David at Jesse's home. David went back to the person who spoke the anointing over his life.

I wonder what David asked of the prophet Samuel.

Hey, man, did you get that anointing thing right, because it sure doesn't seem like it right now?

Listen, Samuel, I love and respect you, but is there any chance you got this wrong?

Did you hear God right?

Did you happen to have a dream about a new king, yet you acted upon it without knowing for sure if it was definitely from God or not?

So many questions. So few details.

We just know David went back to Samuel.

He went to the person who was involved in the calling, the anointing, the favor, the purpose, and the blessing. There was a person who had been involved in laying the foundation for his future, in changing the trajectory of his life, in declaring God's future plans for him, and David had to go back to that place for a reminder.

There was a person and an event David had to fall back on. We have these too.

I bet you can think of a few defining moments in your life. You may not be able to remember the exact day, but I bet you can remember the year, the month, the place, and who was there.

It could be the moment of conversion when you trusted Jesus with your life. Though conversion is often a process that transpires over a season, there is a time, place, and specific people who were involved.

It could be the moment you chose to put the bottle down for good, to step out of an unhealthy, abusive relationship, or the day you chose to leave an unhealthy emotion behind.

It could be a moment of great tragedy and loss, yet your response to it ushered you into hope.

Or maybe you remember having someone of great respect speak and declare a blessing of truth over you. Someone who told you that you mattered, that you will do great things in the world, that you are loved by God, that you have something of worth to offer to the world, or that they see a gift developing in you that will make for a better world.

God's favor, blessing, and anointing come in a variety of ways, but they come. Sometimes they come in thunder, and sometimes in a whisper.

And the beauty of it is that it gives us something to return to so that we are reminded of the touch of God.

It's the place, person, or time when roots were established, cultivated, and strengthened.

✌

Pastor David has been in Barrow a few years. He is one of the most respected pastors in the town. His church had a presence in the local schools, and it was evident that teachers and faculty had great respect for him and his work. I visited his church on Sunday night, and I got to see him pastor his people. I got to see him bear witness to his church about the God who abides, intervenes, and intercedes.

When I arrived in Barrow, I found his name and church through an Internet search, and I emailed him explaining why I was in Barrow. He responded quickly, saying we needed to get lunch, because he had a story to tell me.

At the time, I didn't know that the story he had to tell me was his own story of a journey he had from a dark place, into the light.

We sat down over a pizza in a place overlooking the frozen Arctic Ocean, and after getting to know each other for a few minutes, I began asking more direct questions, and he began to openly share. A while back, as the sun was surfacing again after a couple of months of being absent, he found himself sinking into a dark place. He couldn't put a finger on it. The dark place gave birth to depression, and he couldn't seem to come out of it. The season of darkness he was in became so thick that on Easter Sunday, he announced that he was taking an immediate sabbatical, and he stepped away from ministry, not knowing if he would ever return.

He reached out to a church in Denton, Texas, because he had heard of a pastor who had battled severe depression, and now provided care to tend to the hearts of hurting, broken, and dismantled pastors. Tommy Nelson, the pastor of Denton Bible Church, invited Pastor David and his family to come to Denton for a season of refreshment and to find himself again. So they relocated for a season from Barrow, Alaska, to the Dallas/Fort Worth area. And it was there, slowly, that healing came.

Denton, Tommy Nelson, and Texas had nothing to do with Pastor David's original anointing, calling, or conversion, but it did provide the space for David to be reminded of those exact things. It gave him an atmosphere to reflect on how and where his roots had been established. His time in Denton gave him the energy and passion to return to Barrow with a rejuvenated heart for Jesus and his kingdom.

How to Look Back

Toward the end of my 1995 Ford Ranger's life, the rearview mirror fell off. I didn't realize how often I used it until it was gone. I only went a couple of days without it, but those two days felt like I was a constant safety hazard. Occasionally, I would drive with my left hand on the wheel and my right hand holding up the mirror.

The rearview mirror is a vital part of the vehicle. However, it was created for you to occasionally glance into it. If you stare into it too long, it can be dangerous for you and everyone else around, because you don't know what is in front of you.

Life is the same way. We need moments to reflect on the past, look behind us, and be reminded of what is there and where we have been, but we can't stare too long. There are too many places to go, people to love, and things to do.

I've been involved in a few chip ceremonies at Celebrate Recovery. They celebrate mile-markers in people's road to healing from hurts, habits, and hang-ups. I've noticed that when chip ceremonies are done right, they don't dwell on the past. Instead, they reflect for a moment, and then celebrate the road of freedom that awaits us.

In 1 Samuel, David needed a fresh encounter with Samuel to remind him of his anointing so that he could press forward into the future.

It may be exactly what you need too.

CHAPTER 7

Navigating Life's Transitions

In the unknown, God dwells.

I spoke at an event, and I spent an entire session unpacking that phrase: *in the unknown, God dwells.*

A week later I received a message from a young college student, and it included a picture of her forearm. She had gone to get that phrase tattooed on her body. From her elbow to her wrist was inscribed, *In the unknown, God dwells.* I must say that it is the first and only time I've had someone take a point in my teaching that seriously. I contemplated asking a tattoo artist to set up shop in our lobby at Sycamore View just in case someone wants to go permanent with a point I make each Sunday, but I'm not sure our church would go for it, mostly because there may not be a point I make that is worth it.

It's a phrase a young woman tattooed on her body, but it came after the Lord took a few months to impress those five words on my own heart: *in the unknown, God dwells.*

I was given a sabbatical in the fall of 2015. It was six weeks to catch my breath. I entered it with a vision to absorb some large chunks of Scripture to catch hold of how big, majestic, and brilliant our God is. But I didn't get very far. One chapter in the book of Genesis took hold of my heart and imagination and wouldn't let me go.

In the book of Genesis, things don't go well for brothers. Cain and Abel, Isaac and Ishmael, Jacob and Esau, and Joseph and his brothers—it's a mess! It's the stuff a Jerry Springer show is made of.

Jacob was a twin, and when he was born, he came out of his mother grabbing his brother Esau's heel. His name literally means heel-grabber. Pretty creative, huh? His name is a form of foreshadowing, or so it seems. His life would be a constant wrestling match.

The two brothers grew up with different interests, which doesn't necessarily lead to sibling rivalry. But it does when your parents play favorites, which is exactly what they did. After some deceptive and sketchy actions, Jacob found himself running for his life. Actually, he ran *from* his own home, and ran *to* Uncle Laban's place.

Jacob had two encounters with God in his life. Okay, maybe he had more than that, but we are only told of two. And here's something you need to know about the divine encounters: both happened while Jacob was in the middle of nowhere. He was between places. The second happened in Genesis 32 when he wrestled with God by the river, but the first happened on the way to Uncle Laban's home.

His deceptive behavior had him on the move, having left everything that was familiar. "He came to a certain place and stayed there for the night, because the sun had set. Taking one of the stones of the place, he put it under his head and lay down in that place" (Gen. 28:11).

He used a stone as a pillow. I wonder how much he paused to reflect that night.

> So, this is what my life has become. I'm in the middle of
> nowhere. I can't go back home. I may never see my family

*again. My brother wants to kill me. And this is what my
life has come to. I'm lying down on the ground, using a
stone as a pillow.*

With a stone under his head, he went to asleep, but God didn't
let him sleep through the night. We're told he had a dream. In the
dream, God was right there beside him. And then God spoke. God
didn't speak about how bad Jacob's life had become, but about how
good and faithful God is.

When Jacob woke up, he said, "Surely the LORD is in this
place—and I did not know it! . . . How awesome is this place! This
is none other than the house of God, and this is the gate of heaven"
(vv. 16–17).

It is the first mention of "house of God" in the Bible, and it
wasn't in a building. It was in the in-between, the unknown, and
in a transition.

Then, Jacob made the stone that was a pillow into a pillar. The
stone that reminded him of his failures now became the pillar—the
altar—reminding him of the favor of God. The name of the place
became Bethel—the house of God. When your pillow of stone is
turned into an altar, worship naturally flows.

Bethel became a place Jacob reflected on often. It was there
the Lord established roots, and gave him an encounter to remember for the rest of his life. Roots do that for us. They establish—or
reestablish—our center. They become the anchor we stand on, and
at times, fall back on.

We learn more from how God encountered Jacob than we
do from Jacob. God met him in times of need, and gave him
experiences to testify that when we feel like we are in a season
of unrest, uncertainty, and unfamiliarity, God is nearer than we
could ever imagine.

Interestingly, a couple of decades later, Jacob brought his family back to that exact place to see the stones, and to be reminded of the divine encounter. What God had done for him was a story that needed to be retold for generations to come. God had given him a moment to fall back on, a reminder of a God who wouldn't let him go.

In the unknown, God dwells!

The God of Unexpected Encounters

I boarded a plane in January 2015 from Memphis to Panama City Beach, Florida. For years, I had heard of the Gulf Coast Getaway, an annual worship event for college students, but this would be my first time to attend.

I wasn't sure what I was walking into. I was slated to speak on the opening night. I knew there would be skinny jeans, college sweatshirts, flip-flops, and a few wrist tattoos, but since I was the opening speaker, I wanted to know about the atmosphere, the feel of the room, the energy in hearts, and how spiritually hungry college students would be to discuss things like faith, doubt, and clinging to hope.

I boarded the plane with uncertainty about the event, but in the back of my mind was the uncertainty in my own spirit. I had known for a while that a few unhealthy emotions had been brewing in my heart, yet I kept telling myself that it would be okay, that it wasn't that big a deal, that the good in my heart outweighed the bad, and all that other crap we tell ourselves when we live in denial of the state of our hearts.

So, I got on the plane, drank my Coke Zero (because I pretend to be healthy sometimes), and began looking over my notes for the weekend. One thing I knew was that I didn't want to get in the way of God encountering the precious hearts of eighteen- to twenty-two-year-olds. I knew I wasn't in the healthiest of places, but hey, if God could use a donkey in the Old Testament to relay his message, then he could use me in my brokenness too.

I arrived a few hours before the opening night of worship, and once in the venue, at 6:58, the two-minute countdown began on the screen. It was almost go-time. I knew I wouldn't be up for at least forty-five minutes as we engaged God through praise and song, so I began praying from my seat on the front row, "God, don't hold my sin, my pain, my brokenness, and the unhealthy emotions in my heart against the people here. Use me tonight to bring you glory and to point people to Jesus."

When the countdown was at ten, all thousand-plus people in the room began to scream, "ten . . . nine . . . eight . . . seven," and when it hit zero, the lights went out. I anticipated a worship song with high energy and an upbeat tempo to get the blood flowing in our veins.

Yet that didn't happen.

A young lady and her husband walked to the side of the stage. She got behind a keyboard, and he strapped on his guitar.

And she sang:

Come out of hiding, you're safe here with me.
There's no need to cover what I already see.

With those words, the Lord used this young woman to speak directly into me. God peeled back the outer layer of my heart and mixed conviction with genuine invitation to appeal to me in my weakness.

I began to cry. And I don't cry much. Every once in a while, there's a worship song that touches me so that I get a lump in my throat because it adequately expresses a condition of my heart or the wonder of God in such a way that my body can't help but react.

Later that night, I found the song on iTunes and downloaded it. I had never heard of Steffany Gretzinger before that night, but her song "Out of Hiding" became the most listened-to song on my iPhone over the next few weeks. It wasn't simply because I liked the song, though I did. It's that I needed it. Not like an addict needs a fix, but because in it was the voice of God inviting me to carefully navigate life transitions in a way that helps me become a better man and a more faithful servant.

In January 2015, I wasn't in a valley, but I was on the edge.

I wasn't in a depression, but I was struggling more than ever to live from a place of joy and hope.

My heart was not full of anger and bitterness, but I had allowed those things to become lodged in there, and the cancerous effect was slowly spreading.

I was in a transition—our church was in a transition; Memphis was in a transition—and transitions can strengthen you because you are grounded in the heart and mission of God, or they can slowly turn you into someone you never wanted to become.

How I'm More Like Jacob than I Want to Admit

I began pastoring in Memphis at the Sycamore View Church in 2008. Kayci and I had been married for six years, and our oldest (and only child at the time) had just turned one. He took his first step in Texas, but he began walking in Memphis.

I claim that I was born in Texas, but that Memphis has made me what I am. Kayci doesn't like that claim, because she considers it to be a knock against Texas. (If you didn't know this, Texans love Texas.) What I mean by that statement is that Memphis has taught me so much about the kingdom of God and what it means to joyfully join in systematic and spiritual struggles as we press into the future with hope.

I can honestly say that there have been very few—if any—Sundays that I haven't wanted to join the Sycamore View family to preach a word to them. Very rarely have there been workdays that I didn't want to go. And I can count on one hand how many times I've left an elder's meeting discouraged.

Yet ministry, leading a church, and attempting to be a voice for God in a city can slowly begin to take a toll on you without you even knowing it. Unfortunately, the very things that keep us healthy and rooted in the heart of God are sometimes the first things to be neglected or dismissed as we navigate our way through stress and transitions.

Transitions and all that comes with them aren't foreign to me. And I bet they aren't foreign to you either. What has become evident to me is how important roots are when we face them.

Kayci and I have lived four years of our marriage in Abilene, two in Houston, and now we are going on ten in Memphis. Each move brought change and great challenges.

When we had our first child, we could tag-team, and we could conquer. We were pretty good at two-on-one. Now with two, it is man-to-man coverage, and we've had to learn how to play at a different pace.

When my sister, Jenny, tragically died in February 2010, I found myself in an "in-between place." Strangely, I had never been more convicted that resurrection through Jesus is true, yet I had never been more confused at the intervention of God. The Lord walked with me through that season, and it would later develop into my first book, *Scarred Faith*.

In 2011, our family relocated from the suburbs of Memphis to an under-resourced community, a move that forced us to learn how to faithfully navigate living in a diverse community.

Transitions come in many different forms. Some happen because of job change, marriage, birth, and retirement. Others come in the form of cancer, car wrecks, divorce, adultery, and bankruptcy.

Transitions may not be fun, but they are inevitable. We may not like them, but they often come like pop-up showers; you weren't planning for them, and then all of a sudden you simply find yourself in the midst of one.

Transitions place us in an unknown setting where we aren't sure how the next season of our life will play out, and while we are there, many voices get a chance to speak into our lives and to gain influence. Actually, too many voices get a chance to speak into our lives.

Learning with the Sycamore View Church

God graciously began revealing some brokenness and sin in my life around Thanksgiving 2014. As our church navigated a few transitions, my heart had become vulnerable to unhealthy emotions. My problem—and my ignorance—was that I refused to acknowledge that there was a problem.

I love the Sycamore View Church to the point that I occasionally have to repent before the Lord that it may be idolatry at times. I think God wants us to love the church—and the local church—but not more than we love him. Over the past decade our church family has pressed through some theological, social, and pragmatic shifts.

Our church facility is located in a transient, growingly diverse neighborhood. Our campus sits at the point where the city meets the suburbs. Though our history began as a suburban church, we are no longer one, yet we are not an urban church either. As a church that has felt compelled by God to stay in our location (a story I'll tell in the next chapter), our church demographics have changed significantly. What was once a mid-upper class, white, suburban church has now shifted to become more racially and economically eclectic. It poses beautiful kingdom challenges. I've learned that most people aren't against reconciliation; they just prefer to discuss it in settings where people to their left and right look like them.

In this time, our commitment to the brand name on our church sign declined as we became more and more aware of how big the kingdom of God is. Unfortunately, the tribe that we are a part of has often been known for what we are against more than what we are for. And as is the case for many denominations, getting the Sunday morning worship hour right often outweighs the importance of living right, and faithfully connecting to a community. This theological shift for us was not easy.

As we've grown in areas of confession, expression, and creating space in our worship settings for testimonies, the voices of women began to increase, and as a way to affirm what God was doing, and to root it in the story of Scripture, we engaged in a study of the role of women in public worship, and slowly thereafter, we began implementing a few changes to honor our convictions.

Each shift has been met with great support, encouragement, and affirmation, yet also with pushback, questioning, resistance, and some who chose to no longer journey with us.

I've been a pastor long enough to know that people come and go; that whether we like it or not, the doors of churches are revolving doors. I happen to pastor a church that is in the South, and the reality is that we have a lot of churches down here. In fact, some have said that in Memphis alone, we have more church buildings than gas stations. All that to say, there are a lot of churches to choose from, and a lot of churches to move to when one feels the need for a change.

It's sad, but true, that a lot of church growth that happens in the United States isn't necessarily kingdom growth, it's simply growth by transfer, and at Sycamore View, we've benefited from this throughout the years as much as anyone. Convincing others to leave their church for your church isn't evangelism, and it is rarely good for the kingdom of God. When "Bring a Friend to Church Day" turns into persuading a friend to skip out on their faith community for yours, rarely is good done for the kingdom. I want to help lead a church that grows the way the church in

Acts grew—not by becoming the coolest trend or the church that attracts church people, but by being a church that brings in the people Jesus spent the majority of his time with: the hurting, lost, broken, and fragile.

People sometimes change churches, and it's not because they're bad people. A number of reasons exist, and some of them are healthy reasons. And God has graciously given us the ability to make choices, and to seek him for wisdom and discernment.

For me, what led to some unhealthy emotions wasn't that some people left because of changes we made; it's how they left. It's the names we were called, the snarky Facebook posts, and the unexpected encounters with former members at Kroger who would make snide comments. It was the feelings of betrayal by those who left without even discussing their decisions with me or others: people I baptized, discipled, did weddings for, and funerals for their relatives. It's those who left and actually said, "This place is getting too colorful around here," referring to our growing diversity.

I didn't write this book for pity, or to vent, or to make arguments about not getting my way. I wrote this book because any transition we find ourselves in will shape and form us someway and somehow, either for better or worse. I will talk some about the Sycamore View Church story, because it is one I love, that I'm involved in, and that I believe in. However, this book is much bigger than our story. It's your story. It's learning to faithfully navigate transitions, changes, and shifts.

Without roots, we will spend too much of our lives being reactionary, attempting to develop convictions on the fly. But when we acknowledge the vitality of establishing healthy roots, we become proactive, preparing ourselves to remain connected to God through all of the twists and turns in life.

In my own life, I have navigated the transitions of marriage, parenting, moving into a new city, walking with grief, getting serious about unhealthy emotions and rhythms, and leading a church. Your journey is not my journey, but the life journey we are on is similar.

I love the church, and I want you to love it too. With all of her warts and black eyes, she is God's hope for the world. The church is made up of people. Broken people. Messy people. Yet people who are dearly loved by God. And sometimes the people who step on stage week after week are those battling the greatest demons that have the power to cause destruction. The enemy of God knows that if he can begin to rob leaders (or any Christ-follower) of joy and hope, he can slowly weaken their witness to the world. When joy and hope wane, bitterness and resentment step into their place.

Which is why I felt the nudge of God, or the invitation of God, in November 2014 to take some time to allow him to weed out the unrighteous anger and bitterness that was slowly beginning to take over my heart.

I've come to realize that anger rarely hijacks a heart overnight. It prefers to function like a slow drip, like an IV. A little here. A little there. And when the drip continues for weeks, months, or a few years without any soul care, it has the crafty ability to slowly turn any human into someone they never wanted to be.

So, when I felt God inviting me to allow him to take it from me, I resisted. If it's possible, I gave God a stiff arm. It was as if I told him, "God, seriously, I'm fine. It's not as big a deal as you're making it out to be. I'm just fine."

Anger had lodged itself in a corner of my heart, and the pain was slowly spreading. I wanted to manage the pain. In some weird way, maybe there was a part of it that I liked.

Yet, six weeks later, I found myself in Florida at Gulf Coast Getaway, the conference with college students, in desperate need of an intervention of God.

And the line from the song, "Come out of hiding, you're safe here with me," ushered me into the presence of God to be sifted, transformed, and tended to.

That weekend, I also had dinner one night with my good friend Dave Clayton. I confessed to him what was taking place inside me, and he also pointed me, as Dave often does, to a place in Scripture for a word of hope and healing. James 3:14 says, in effect, "Do not harbor bitter envy or selfish ambition." And Dave reminded me how a harbor works. It is a small part of a body of water protected and deep enough for ships to anchor for safe shelter from storms.

When anger—or any unhealthy emotion—lodges itself in our heart, a harbor can be constructed that holds in the unhealthy emotion, and keeps the waves of God from getting in.

Do we trust God enough to allow him to begin to break down the harbors that we've created in our lives?

What hit me that weekend was that I could no longer move forward in life without a change of heart. Holding on to my anger would slowly lead to a pathless life. And I knew I didn't want that. Kayci and my boys don't deserve that. Neither does the Sycamore View Church.

I needed God to help me navigate life, not perfectly, but faithfully. And I bet you do too.

Transitions are navigated best when our roots are well established.

It's time for the pillows of stone to become our pillars that declare the faithfulness of God.

CHAPTER 8

Healthy Roots Produce Joy

I started a few fights between married couples not too long
ago. And it was from something I said in my sermon.

I've said things before that have caused one spouse to elbow
the other. Statements like:

Do we have any hoarders in the house today?

*How many of you can go from calm to red-hot anger
by the simple sound of a Cheerio crunching under your
child's foot while walking through the kitchen?*

*If you have more than thirty pairs of shoes in your closet,
you may be in bondage.*

*Do you know someone who reflects the fruit of the Spirit
in almost every area of their life except when they drive?*

The fight I started in May 2015 wasn't one of those kinds
of statements.

My friend Mike Cope, the director of the annual Pepperdine
Lectures, had asked me to give the opening keynote message at the

Pepperdine Lectures. The text I was given to preach from was James 1:1–18, and he specifically wanted me to focus on James 1:2–4, "My brothers and sisters, whenever you face trials of any kind, consider it nothing but joy, because you know that the testing of your faith produces endurance; and let endurance have its full effect, so that you may be mature and complete, lacking in nothing."

I've always had a love-hate relationship with James 1:2–4. At times, it provides strength to keep going and not give up. Then, there are times I read it and think, *You got some guts, James. Seriously? Joy through suffering? Your momma can consider it nothing but joy!* But since his mom is Mary the mother of Jesus, I probably need to stay away from the "your momma" jokes.

I wasn't sure how to the end the message. I talked a lot that night about protecting our joy and clinging to it, but I wasn't sure how to land the plane. And if you've been to church a few times before, you've probably heard a preacher who didn't know how to land the plane, so he or she kept circling the airport like fifteen times. And if you're a pastor reading this, wondering what I'm talking about, you're probably the one who circles the airport a dozen times every Sunday.

Since I was preaching during a season in which my joy had taken a hit, I was vulnerable about my own journey. So, I ended the sermon by creating a time of prayer for joy. We do this at Sycamore View quite often, and it has become part of our church culture. The beauty of it is that sometimes we simply create space for God to work and then we watch him move in transforming ways. The challenge and anxiety come because, what if you create a time of prayer and people don't move, or they just don't get it?

I specifically asked for church leaders, pastors, and elders who were struggling to live and lead from a place of joy to stand. Maybe their joy had taken a hit; maybe it was barely hanging on by a thread. I'm convinced that leaders must lead from a place of joy if we want any shot at impacting others. People may follow a joyless person for a season, but they won't for a lifetime.

As they began to stand, I followed that up by asking others who were in need of joy to stand.

I wasn't sure what would happen or if anything would happen. I've come to rest in the fact that in these moments, success is not determined by how many people stand, but by being obedient to God and trusting that he's working in hearts even when we can't see it.

But that night, people began to stand. And people surrounded them. Pockets of prayer filled the gymnasium, and prayer broke out.

I would later find out that a few fights began between spouses, because there were those nudging their husbands, saying, "You need to stand up."

"No, I'm fine."

"You know you need to. The stress of church leadership is robbing you of joy, and you know it."

"I know, but I'm embarrassed to stand."

"You better stand right now to receive this blessing from the Lord."

"Shut up."

"No! You shut up! And stand!"

It's not just true for faith leaders, but for all Jesus people in general: if we lose our joy, we lose our witness. Period.

The Church and the City

At Sycamore View, we talk about the encounter between Jesus and Zacchaeus quite a bit (Luke 19:1–10). One reason is that we think the story has a lot to say to us today, and the other reason is that our church's permanent address is 1910 Sycamore View Road. In Luke 19, Zacchaeus climbed a sycamore tree, and Jesus says that he came to seek and save the lost. You get why this story means a lot to us?

In the late 1970s, we were a church that relocated to what was then the outskirts of Memphis. The leaders were working out of their best understanding of the gospel, and their attempts to make an impact in their current transient, changing community were creating more challenges for them. They didn't know what to do, so they gave their building to an African American church, and moved farther out.

In the 1980s, the church grew. It had an attractive facility, and more importantly, one of the most vibrant and compelling youth groups in the area.

The numerical growth continued into the 1990s, and a couple of preachers came along who taught Scripture in a way that was different. By different, I mean they taught about a relationship with God, and not just rules and regulations. Sadly, in many faith tribes, people are their church brand-name first, and Christians second. The '90s broke people out of that.

In 2001, our attendance reached an all-time high. A big reason was the post–9/11 effect, which caused many Americans to search for hope, reality, and destiny.

It was about that time that people at Sycamore View began questioning whether it was time to relocate or not. The suburbs had moved miles beyond our church facility, and the neighborhood was trending toward greater racial and economic diversity.

As faithful leaders should, our leaders entered into a season of prayer and fasting, and the decision was made to stay in our current location. Moving farther out didn't settle well in their spirits. Staying put seemed like the most God-honoring thing to do.

This commitment to stay at 1910 Sycamore Road wasn't enough for some people. We had committed followers of Jesus who began praying big, bold prayers that God would teach us to love our neighbors, and that he would open doors for us to connect with our community in ways that would change it, and us.

This was the vision that captured Kayci and me when we were invited to interview in 2008. At the time, I was pastoring a church in Houston, and we loved it. We didn't have plans to move. Yet Sycamore View called not once, or twice, but three times. One phone call alone caused us to entertain the conversation. A grandfather in the faith to me, Lynn Anderson, who at the time was an elder at the Oak Hills Church in San Antonio, had done some consulting with the elders and leaders at Sycamore View, and he encouraged me to engage in a dialogue because he thought our gifts and passions would fit well in a Memphis context. Lynn is one of the few people in my life for whom, if he asked me to walk from Memphis to San Antonio to visit with him, I would begin walking tomorrow. That is the love and respect I have for him.

When we arrived in Memphis to interview, before we were shown the church facility, we were taken on a tour of the community and city we were called to serve and walk alongside of. The mission of God was placed in front of us before the church facility.

It was compelling to hear of a church that intentionally chose to stay in a location and to press back into a city. It was inspiring to hear that they were eager to have a preacher who could help them learn how to love a community the way Jesus would.

A church that is willing to take risks is a church I am willing to learn from and press into. Playing it safe was never a motto or a phrase used to describe the mission of the church. And I don't ever want to be known as that kind of person.

We came to Memphis knowing that there would be challenges. And there have been plenty. Yet where there are challenges, one will also find an enormous amount of God's grace and activity.

❧

I spent time with a few churches while in Barrow. I had a chance to sit with pastors and hear countless stories. The churches I visited were small, yet close-knit. They were family. Over and over I heard the phrase, "We need each other." And that's a phrase that goes all the way back to the book of Acts, right?

One afternoon, I helped the leader of a church unload tables from the bed of a truck. After carrying them inside to their fellowship area, we stood by a heater to warm our hands. I asked questions. He talked. I listened. It was interesting to hear him talk about what happens to the church when the sun reappears in late January. It grows. People come back. They return. It's not that they took time off from God, but the darkness and cold often keeps people inside. Yet when the sun is back, the church experiences life and energy again. I like that. The light exists for the church to thrive.

When the Church Is On
I love the church!

When the church is on, there is nothing in the world that is more redemptive, healing, and life-giving. It is unlike any force the world has ever seen.

A heavenly vision requires a newly formed community that reflects the character, nature, and behavior of heaven. It is a community where barriers and dividing walls are torn down, favoritism isn't allowed, and where a new ethic is embraced as the path of deeper entry into God's heart and mission for the world.

In the church, there is no room for economic favoritism, pervasive racial tension, and long-standing division that keeps the voices and gifts of women silent when the people of God get together for a formative time of worship.

As Scripture unveils God's desire for reconciliation, it is clear that it is something that God desires between himself and people, but it is more than that. It is something that God desires between people. Reconciliation is vertical and horizontal.

There are pragmatic reasons to live into God's future, but there are also theological reasons.

Some warn against diversifying your church racially, economically, or with female participation. Ed Stetzer once noted, "Everybody wants diversity, but many don't want to be around people who are different." Most people I know are proponents of reconciliation, but in the church, you'll find many who are for it, but they prefer to discuss it in settings where others look like them, live like them, and smell like them.

However, we need another way. For what awaits us one day is a day of great inclusion and celebrated diversity.

I once heard a good friend say, "We have too many fences in our world. We need more bridges."

It's time for the church to get into the bridge-building business.

Faithfulness at All Costs

To commit to deep forms of reconciliation is also a commitment to change and transition. I have a friend who said that we need to quit leading our churches as if the sign out front says, "Been Keeping the Joneses Happy for 40 Years," and we need to study Scripture to see what kind of community God is forming now.

I'm not a proponent of changing for the sake of change, but I also believe that change is mandatory for growth and development.

Fear has held the church back in far too many areas of life, and it still does. Fear is an emotion created by God, but it was never meant to be a controlling device. Through any change and/or transition, fear speaks loudly, yet it must be drowned out by a commitment to faithfulness.

Faithfulness at all costs.

Faithfulness no matter what the price.

Faithfulness even when it hurts.

Joy Is a Choice

The speaking engagement at Pepperdine received more responses than any other I've had. I was shocked—and maybe I shouldn't have been—at how many people have either lost their joy or are close to losing it. People reached out to me, not as a joy expert, but as people who were in need of a friend. They confessed to losing their joy for ministry, the church, their cities, and life in general.

When roots are established correctly—which means they are firmly planted in the heart and mission of God—fruit comes naturally. You don't have to see the roots of a tree to determine if it is a healthy tree. The fruit of the tree reveals that. You don't have to see the roots to tell if fruit is ripe. Just look at the fruit.

In the same way, we shouldn't have to go into details with people about how our roots have been established, because the fruit should be doing the talking.

Joy is one of the prerequisites for change, transformation, evangelism, and growth. People do not want to follow or listen to joyless people, and if they do, it's not God or the things of God they are after.

After my speaking engagement at Pepperdine, I received many calls from people confessing how they were losing joy, and I told them the same thing I need to remind myself of every day:

Wake up and choose joy.

Believe that joy is greater than despair.

Cling to joy as if it is a priceless treasure.

Trust that the joy of the Lord transcends all things.

Live each day believing that joy and hope are worth fighting for.

PART 3

Rhythm

When I was a sophomore at Abilene Christian University, a group of friends traveled to the Dallas/Fort Worth area one weekend. On Saturday night, we attended a Fort Worth Brahmas minor league hockey game.

During the first intermission, as music played, the twenty of us were having a little too much fun with the music. We turned our section into an all-out dance party. Little did we know that an employee for the Brahmas had spotted us while we were cutting up and having a good time.

As the game resumed, the woman in charge of entertainment came over and asked if one of us would like to participate in a dance competition during the second intermission. Her invitation came with the guarantee of a nice prize for the winner. Being one who has often day-dreamed about being in a Justin Timberlake

music video, or becoming a member of the Jabbawockeez, I didn't hesitate to raise my hand. Looking back, I can't remember if it was the opportunity to dance in front of the crowd or the opportunity to win a prize that was more appealing. However, I threw her off when I said, "Ma'am, I'll do this under one condition. I'm here with some of my friends from college. Would it be okay for them to come down and surround us during the competition?"

Not only did she agree, but she said she would do something better than that. She would put where we were from up on the Jumbotron.

Little did I know how well we were about to represent our university . . . or something like that.

The second intermission began, and they introduced the candidates over the sound system:

"And another one of our contestants is Josh Ross, a Bible major, from Abilene Christian University."

The music began, and I danced my face off. For 90 seconds, I gave it all I had.

To determine the winner, the emcee put her hand over each contestant, and the crowd cheered for whoever they thought won. And believe it or not, the crowd cheered the loudest for me.

I won.

"And we have a winner! Josh Ross, the Bible major, from Abilene Christian University, and he has just won a $20 gift certificate to . . ."

And they mentioned a prominent one-word sports bar that my wife would *not* appreciate me going to.

What am I going to do with *that* gift certificate?

I went home and told my parents, and my mom framed the certificate on the wall. I'm not sure if she framed it because she was so proud of me, or because she knew that if she framed it I couldn't use it.

You may have two left feet, but I bet you know something about dancing and rhythm.

My kids love to dance. It doesn't matter if music comes on at a Grizzlies' basketball game, a restaurant, during a commercial, at a bowling alley, or even in Target, they begin to move to the sound, and it almost seems like it is an innate reaction, more than a conscious choice. It's almost as if moving to the sound of music is in their bones from birth.

Can you think of any culture in the world in which it is not okay for children to dance? When children dance, adults pull out their phones and begin to make videos to send to relatives and put on Facebook. We laugh, gather a crowd, and ask them to do it again.

There is a rhythm that is planted deep in our DNA. There is a rhythm in the way your heart beats, your lungs breathe, and your eyes blink.

My friends in Barrow spoke a lot about *rhythm*. In the wintertime, it is a healthy rhythm that keeps people warm, sharp, on their toes, joyful, and active. In the summertime when the sun rarely sets, it is rhythm that keeps people rested, well nourished, and consistent.

There is also a rhythm in our soul. There is a rhythm in our walk with God.

God invites us into it.

In fact, Jesus had it. Maybe you have never thought about Jesus having rhythm, but let me show you how he did.

Henri Nouwen refers to Luke 6:12–18 as the Jesus Rhythm, or the Jesus Paradigm. In 6:12, Jesus spent the night in prayer with God. The next morning, he called together the twelve apostles. This was immediately followed by a season of teaching, healing, and driving out demons.

Solitude. Community. Ministry.

This three-part rhythm kept Jesus rooted in God's heart, God's community, and God's mission. It was the rhythm that Jesus handed on to his followers, and the rhythm that we see in the early church.

Solitude. Community. Ministry.

It was a rhythm of plugging into the heart and character of God, because it is our source of strength.

It was a rhythm that kept people plugged in to meaningful relationship, because with God there is no such thing as a Lone Ranger Christian, and God rarely called (or calls) people into solo missions.

And it was a rhythm that kept people plugged in to compassion, justice, and service.

When these three are meshing well, maturity, growth, and development take place. The kingdom of God advances in a heart, and in the world.

Yet, when one, two, or all three are neglected for a lengthy season, growth can be set back, and our faith in God can be misaligned.

Rhythm is vital for life, and for reentry.

It's important in Barrow.

It's important where you live too.

So, let's dance!

CHAPTER 9

Reimagining Solitude

Occasionally I get the sense that God is inviting me into a season of exploring and redirecting my heart. It's not an audible voice I hear, but a strong conviction. It's the kind of conviction that makes you really pay attention.

In January 2013, I was leaving Memphis for a weekend outside of Tampa when I felt this invitation. I remember praying as I walked into the airport early that morning that God would help me to pay attention throughout the weekend. I wanted my heart to be centered. Even if there were pieces of my heart that needed to be destroyed or rebuilt, I was willing to lie on my face and let it happen, because I now know that God has my best interests in mind. He goes after the priorities and convictions of our hearts, not to destroy us, but because he cares about us.

As I boarded the plane, I took a moment to pray and discern whether it was an "ear-bud-in" or an "ear-bud-out" flight. In other words, could I put my ear buds in and keep to myself, or did I need to attempt to engage the person next to me in conversation to see if it led to Jesus and the kingdom? Some of you reading this chapter are probably those people who put the ear buds in on a plane, not because you're desperate to listen to music, but because you immediately want others to know you are off limits. Some of you are the chatterboxes others see coming from a mile away. You are a dialogue waiting to happen.

I sensed that it needed to be an ear-bud-out flight, so I began to engage the woman next to me in a conversation. Within the first ninety seconds, we went deep. She began to share that because of a midlife crisis and some depression, her family had moved to the coast in Florida. I thought to myself, "Maybe I should have listened to music, because I did not go to seminary to walk women through menopause. I'm not trained in this." Yet I remained present in the conversation.

From Memphis to Atlanta, we talked about pain and hope; brokenness and faith. Our conversation was coming to an end as we approached the runway, but our plane went back up in the air as the pilot said, "We need to circle the airport for a few moments. There has been a miscommunication. We will be back down in just a few minutes." But we didn't circle the airport. For the next twenty-five minutes, we flew in the opposite direction from Atlanta. Passengers began growing restless as we looked at each other and attempted to get answers from the flight attendants. Then, as the plane began to turn around, the pilot came back on, and he didn't hold anything back, "We have a little problem," he said. "The front wheel of the plane won't come out. We think it may come out, but we aren't sure if it's going to lock. However, we have been given permission to land the plane, and in the event the wheel doesn't lock, the plane will slide on its belly until we come to a stop. Emergency crews and fire trucks will be on the ground to assist us if there is a problem. We should be fine. Our flight attendants are going to take a few moments to walk you through emergency landing positions."

Emergency landing position?!?!?!

It sounded way too much like "emergency *crash* position!"

They coached and we listened. Arms crossed in front of you. Forehead needs to touch the seat in front of you. Wait until you are told to get in position.

At this point the midlife crisis lady was comforting me. Someone else said, "Hey, you're a pastor, right? Can't you do something?" They were half joking, but I wasn't sure how to respond. What could I do? I could begin praying, but I wasn't even sure what to begin rebuking.

As we neared the ground, I thought that I might need to take a moment to say good-bye to my family. This could be it. I thanked God for my amazing wife. We were just a few months away from celebrating our eleventh year of marriage. She's the best thing that has ever happened to me. I gave thanks for my two boys. Because I was possibly laying my final requests before the Lord, I remember even thinking, "God, keep them strong. Mature them to be your people in the world. Keep them from ever loving cats more than dogs. And please don't allow them to grow up to be SEC fans. Those people annoy me. Please honor these requests." I didn't hold anything back.

The flight attendants yelled for us to get in our positions. We did. Arms crossed. Lean forward. Forehead touching seat. You could hear a pin drop. And my final thought was this, "Don't scream like a girl. Don't scream like a girl." I didn't want there to be one survivor, and when interviewed on CNN by Anderson Cooper about what he remembered from the crash, say, "All I remember is that there was one guy in seat 22D who was screaming for his mommy. I will remember that grown man's high-pitched shrill for the rest of my life."

The plane landed, fire trucks were cruising down the runway next to us, and thankfully, it was the smoothest landing I've ever had. When we came to a stop, we applauded and gave each other hugs and high fives. I chest-bumped the pilot, which he did not appreciate. We walked off the plane and hugged the walls. We were alive!

After texting my wife, family, and close friends about my "near-death" experience, I thought about the prayer time I had with God earlier that morning. I felt like there were some things God needed to do in my heart that weekend, and if he didn't have my attention before the flight, he did now.

You know, I don't think God created that flight experience just for me. I think God is more creative than that. But I do think God can take experiences in our lives and use them for his purposes. As I honored silence and solitude throughout that weekend, God revealed places in my heart that needed to change. There were insecurities that had been growing in me that I wasn't even aware of. I just needed to be still so they could be revealed.

Changing Gears

Have you ever had a moment when an author, pastor, teacher, motivational speaker, or a leader of any kind spoke a word of truth into your life with such direct power that you wanted to kick them in their shin because it hurt so bad?

Archbishop William Temple once said, "Your religion is what you do with your solitude." Doesn't that make you just want to scream? Yet, it is so true.

We are told that Jesus often went to lonely places to be alone with God (Luke 5:16). It was vital to his health, development, and relationship to his Father.

Since my 1995 Ford Ranger died (which I still don't want to talk about), I've been driving a 2009 Honda Civic Hybrid. I like it. However, some of my Texas friends have de-friended me because of it. In fact, one friend told me that I now drive a suppository on wheels. Yet, here's the deal: whenever my car gets close to empty, I stop and fill it up with gas. Every time. I did this when I had my truck too. When it was close to empty, I filled it up. I really don't have to sit around discerning whether to put gas in it or not. It's what I do. It's what you do too.

When it's time for an oil change, I take it to the Midas down from our church facility. When a check engine light comes on, I usually ignore it for a few days, waiting to see if it will go off on its own, but when it doesn't, then I take it in to get checked out. After a drive into Texas to see family, I clean the windshield.

A few months ago, it hit me . . . why does it seem we take better care of our vehicles than we do of our souls? We often live such panicked, hurried, broken lives that we don't even know how to take care of ourselves. Solitude is the discipline of getting away, but who has time to do that, right? We know flight attendants prepare passengers on every flight that in case of a sudden drop in cabin pressure, an oxygen bag will fall from above, and to make sure you put it on yourself first before helping others. *Take care of yourself first, so you can take care of others.* Yet do we believe the same logic translates into life?

Too often our hearts get close to empty, and we tell ourselves we can make it a few more months until the holidays.

Our faith vision becomes cloudy, and we attempt to convince ourselves we really aren't that bad.

There may be a rip or tear in our life with God or with others, and we think that if we simply keep it from getting worse, we will be just fine.

Something in our lives begins to smell like dog mess, and we simply spray perfume on it, thinking it may get rid of the smell.

Taking time to reflect on, inspect, and take inventory of the condition of our heart can be a painful step toward greater health, maturity, and joy; yet it may be the best step we could ever make.

∾

One day a couple of my friends in Barrow and I sat in a quiet place discussing rhythm. They shared how vital rhythm is to the health of the community, and I shared about Luke 6 and Jesus's rhythm of solitude, community, and ministry. I asked a few direct questions about solitude because I was really curious about what that looked like for them in their context, especially in the wintertime.

One friend had asked the city for money to build an ice rink so he could teach hockey to kids. It was a way to keep kids active, and it was also a ministry for him. Because there are no roads leading out of town, flying is the only way to play games against opponents. So recreational hockey becomes a traveling event. Traveling takes time. Time means people are together. And that makes for opportunities for meaningful ministry.

When he asked the mayor for money, part of his plan was that he would keep the ice smooth and clean. An ice resurfacer was purchased, and this became a valuable place for my friend to connect with the Lord. Multiple times a week, it was just an ice resurfacer and him. No distractions. Very little noise. Solitude.

Whether we know it or not, our souls crave it.

Two things make me nervous about solitude.

One, what if nothing happens? What if I don't feel anything? Will I keep coming back?

Two, what if something does happen? What if God does begin to speak, convict, poke, prod, and disassemble? Then what?

A Place to Begin

I meet with the Celebrate Recovery group at Sycamore View a few times a year. Occasionally, I've had the honor (and challenge) of teaching Step 4: *make a searching and fearless moral inventory of yourself*. It's one of the most gut-wrenching and soul-searching lessons for me to teach at CR, because it forces me to take seriously what this step may do to me. Sometimes I don't want to see what's under the hood. I don't want to know what needs to change.

Jesus often withdrew to lonely places to pray, Luke tells us.

Luke tells us that honoring meaningful solitude was vital to Jesus's rhythm, and maybe it should be for us too.

A lot of times when I travel to speak, I walk people through Luke 6:12–19 and the Jesus Rhythm of solitude, community, and ministry. I ask people which one comes easiest to them and which presents the greatest challenge. Hands down, solitude is the greatest challenge.

Without solitude, there can be no reflection, inspection, and inventory. And without them, there can be no growth, maturity, or development.

John Ortberg, a well-known pastor and best-selling author, wrote an article for *Christianity Today*, which later worked its way into his book *Soul Keeping*. The rhythm of John's life had become quite chaotic, and he phoned a friend (Dallas Willard) to gauge the health of his heart. After a long pause, Willard slowly responded, "You must ruthlessly eliminate hurry from your life." Ortberg scribbled it down and then waited for Step #2. What was the next thing Willard would suggest he do? But there was another long pause. Willard stated, "There is nothing else. You must ruthlessly eliminate hurry from your life."[1]

We may think our spiritual lives need something deep and profound—like a conference or a concert that we could attend, another book to read, more service, more services—the list can go on and on; but don't underestimate rest and solitude. They are necessary components of a rhythm that protects longevity, and without it, burnout persists, and the shallow waters are as deep as we will ever go.

Here are a few of the primary challenges that keep us from enjoying and protecting meaningful solitude.

We live under the illusion that we are busy people. Yet, in reality, we are more distracted than we are busy. Voices, noises, rings, text message dings, and a variety of images are constantly vying for our attention and affection. I talk with people regularly who admit how they are struggling in their prayer life because they can't pay attention. How many times have you sat down to pray, and within the first sixty seconds, you are bombarded with your to-do list, a phone call you need to make, an errand you forgot to run, a text you need to respond to, or that you forgot to start the dishwasher? Too many of us don't sit still through the initial wave of distractions for our hearts to settle in with God.

I often encourage people to develop a prayer life where you connect with God in a room or space away from your phone. Try it sometime.

There are times when Kayci and I are talking, yet she can see that I'm distracted by ESPN, a phone, a computer, or a thought, and she will say, "Josh, I need you to listen to me with your eyes!" Focus. Give attention. Stay in the moment.

One of the greatest gifts we have to offer God and people is being fully present, available, and attentive.

We are physically and emotionally exhausted. The mixture of a distracted and exhausted heart can be lethal for the health of our hearts. I'm not saying anything is impossible with God, yet I must ask, how is God going to speak a clear word into a distracted, exhausted heart?

Developing an unhealthy pace in life comes easier than we might think. In a sermon I preached a couple of years ago, I actually put someone on a treadmill on the stage during my message. I started the treadmill on a slow pace . . . a stroll. Then I began to hand him items. A backpack. A football. Weights. A to-go bag from Chick-fil-A (because everyone needs some Christian chicken, right?) A photo album. And more. Then I cranked the treadmill up to a pretty good jog. Keep in mind, I made Seth King (my willing volunteer) sign a waiver beforehand just in case of an injury. The point being that unhealthy paces are easily developed, and it stunts our growth in Christ, as well as keeps us from loving others extravagantly.

God created rest for a reason. Our bodies were not made to need substances to go to bed, and caffeine to give us an adrenaline boost in the morning.

Jesus was in demand, on the move, and more balanced in life than we could ever imagine, and yet he was determined to honor time to get alone to be with God. What can we do?

How do we handle stress management? I was recently challenged to focus more on energy management and stress management than on time management. One of the reasons we struggle with reflection, inspection, and inventory is that we live life under an overwhelming cloud of stress.

Do you have activities or projects in your life that take up time, yet don't drain you of emotional energy? On the flip side, do you have activities or projects that don't take up much time, yet they use up a lot of emotional energy?

The question I tend to ask people is this: *What role do you invite God to play in how you handle stress and energy management?*

Are we willing to press through growing pains to mature? Occasionally when I have taken my car in for a routine oil change, a mechanic will ask me if I want to get other stuff worked on. I'm so vulnerable in these situations, because I know nothing about cars, and I don't really care to learn. I don't know if they are changes I really need or not.

Would you like a new air filter . . . tire rotation . . . water pump . . . this . . . that . . . ?

I don't know if I do or don't.

A couple of times I've been asked, "Would you like for us to do an alignment check?"

Usually I say no. And the main reason why is that if I need further work, I don't want to know about it because I don't want to know what it costs.

We don't want to know what is broken, because the cost of fixing it may take sacrifice. Sound familiar?

This is true in so many areas of life. Growing may cause pain, but it's the only way to development and maturity. Are we willing to work through the mess in order to live into the best?

We are spiritually malnourished. Being nurtured back to health takes discipline, exercise, rhythm, and a better diet. A few years back, a friend of mine told me he was upset with his doctor because the doctor demanded that he lose weight, exercise more, and eat much healthier. I asked him what he's going to do about it, and he said, "Well, I got a new doctor."

Just as what we take into our bodies has an impact on our health, what we take into our heart has an impact on both our health and our ability to produce fruit.

Fruit doesn't come from trees that are not properly nurtured. And so it is with our hearts too.

Unfortunately, we can live in denial about our sin and insecurities, as well as in denial about the seriousness of our need for change. This is what Dallas Willard called "the gospel of sin management." It's when we convince ourselves that if we can just manage sin by keeping it contained, then we can keep it from getting out of control.

Have you ever realized how dangerous many of our worship lyrics are? In fact, we often sing more lies than we speak. We sing some radical stuff in our worship gatherings. We sing about giving God our all, our sins being washed clean, turning our eyes to Jesus, that Jesus is all we need, etc. Are we willing to live into the words we sing to God?

One of the most interesting components of the seven deadly sins is that they don't seem so deadly. Pride, envy, anger, sloth, greed, gluttony, lust . . . sounds like what drives the American economy to me, right? It sounds like what we watch every week on soap operas, *The Bachelor*, on billboards, the radio, and in the heated 2016 presidential election.

Think about it. In the seven deadly sins, there is no mention of alcohol, but there is of overeating. No mention of murder, but there is of sloth. And apparently your fantasies about Nicole Kidman are worse than Hitler's genocide.

They seem so ordinary and unspectacular. They're personal, individual, but they also seem so small. Can these things really compete with sexism, racism, violence, etc.?

One of the temptations in life is to keep sin large, global, universal, and out there! Keep the focus on ISIS, DC, marriage equality, and those over there. It's much easier to point out the sins in others than it is to get real about the sin in me.

Before Augustine—one of the most revered church leaders of all time—knew God, he was a womanizer. He had a child out of wedlock and hinted at many youthful adventures. But you know what convicted him and set him on a course for God? He stole some pears off a neighbor's tree. And it was that small act that convicted him to the core.

The seven deadly sins are deadly, not because they lead directly to damnation, but because they slowly rot the soul! They are so ordinary, so pervasive, that we often fail to see how much they warp our minds and hearts. They first appear as harmless, but then they grow up and cause great harm. And once they get hold of you, they are extremely difficult to shake.

There is no such thing as a secret sin that doesn't have a profound impact on everyone else around you. The attempt to manage sin stunts growth and keeps us from development.

The first mention of "sin" in the New Testament is in Matthew 1:21, and it isn't what sin does to people, but what Jesus came to do to sin.

As there is fear in going under the knife, there is also fear of having our hearts examined. One thing I've learned over the past few years is that surgeons don't perform surgery on moving people. Dentists don't pull wisdom teeth while patients play PS3. Appendixes aren't removed while people are scooting around in a shopping mall. Patients need to be completely still. Anesthetics aren't just for the benefit of the patient. They are just as much for surgeons and nurses. For the health of our hearts and for the hope of the world, God needs us to learn to be still.

It is possible to miss out on the blessings of God because we aren't able to pay attention to the gift.

Slow down.

Rest well.

Breathe deeply.

Enjoy God.

Note

[1]John Ortberg, "Ruthlessly Eliminate Hurry," CT Pastors, July 2002, accessed February 17, 2017, http://www.christianitytoday.com/pastors/2002/july-online-only /cln20704.html/.

CHAPTER 10

Reimagining Community

Researching light, darkness, roots, and rhythm led me to a town in Norway called Rjukan. All I really know about Norway is that it is somewhere over there, up there, and yonder. I think cold, skiing, bobsledding, and blond-haired people.

There are similarities between Barrow and Rjukan. Both are small. Neither is a famous vacation spot. And both get cold. However, they are quite different. Specifically, they are different in how they are forced to deal with darkness and light. Let me explain.

Rjukan is a relatively young town. It celebrated its hundredth birthday not long ago. Founded in the early 1900s by a man named Samuel Eyde, it would become home to the world's first large-scale fertilizer plant. Samuel (known as Uncle Sam) was an industrialist, a scientist, a creator, and an artist. With his vision, drive, and expertise, Uncle Sam was able to harness power from a hundred-meter waterfall to generate hydroelectric power. At the time, it was the world's largest power plant.

The town became famous for its innovation and technology. But there was one thing they couldn't do. They couldn't change the elevation of the sun.

It's a town of 3,500 people, and they live in the shadows six months of the year. Late September to mid-March, it isn't dark like Barrow and other towns above the Arctic Circle that go without the sun for a period of time, but it's not bright either. Rjukan is located in a valley surrounded by mountains. From the town, people can see that the sun is on the other side of the mountain, but they can't see it for itself. And over time, this messes with people.

One person said, "The sun is right there, so close you can almost touch it."

And yet another Rjukan resident, "We'd look up and see blue sky above, and the sun high on the mountain slopes, but the only way we could get to it was to go out of town. The brighter the day, the darker it was down here. And it's sad, a town that people have to leave in order to feel the sun."

And that's what they have to do. They have to leave their home and climb the side of the mountain, in order to see the sun.

In 1928, they built a cable car, which still exists today. For a small fee, it carries people to the top of the mountain, where they can sip coffee and catch a majestic view of the rays of the sun.

One person said, "Living in the shade must make you afraid to dream of the sun. Like the valley walls, minds without sun become somehow a little bit narrower."[1]

That phrase wouldn't let me go: *minds without sun become somehow a little bit narrower.*

Living in the shadows!

I wonder how often we settle for the shade and shadows instead of taking the ride to see the light.

Much like the cable cars in Rjukan, the local church has been tasked to carry people from the shadows to the light. People in Rjukan trust the cable cars to carry them to a place for healing, therapy, joy, and adventure. Do people in the world and in our current culture trust the church enough to carry them somewhere? And if not, what must we do to repair broken trust?

Don't Do That with Your Body

When the church is on, there is nothing more redemptive, beautiful, and healing in the world. Yet when the church is off, we can cause great damage.

Luke Norsworthy has been one of my closest friends since college.[2] One summer during seminary, we took an intensive short course together. It's a one-week, five-day, 8:00–5:00 class. Each day when class was over, we went to the gym to release the tension from a long day of New Testament Theology, because few things go together like stair-climbers, bench press, exegesis, and the primary threads running through the synoptic Gospels, right?

On the second day of class, Luke decided take his chest work to another level. After propping his feet against a wall, he placed his hands in two stirrups hanging from a machine, and proceeded to do a few air push-ups. But that wasn't enough for him. Wanting to take it up a notch, he hung a seventy-five-pound dumbbell around his neck and did a few more. When he finished, he felt a twitch in his neck, but didn't think anything of it.

The next morning during class, he sneezed, and when he did, something happened. He whispered to me, "Boss." (A lot of friends call me Boss. Not because I'm bossy, but because it rhymes: Josh the Boss Ross.) "Boss, the left side of my face just went numb." He walked out of class. An hour later, I called him on our lunch break, and he asked if I could hurry and pick him up and drive him to the emergency room.

When I drove up to his home, he walked out holding a trash can. This wasn't good. I've already told you that my greatest phobia in life is throw-up. I don't do well with it. I'm better since becoming a dad, but I don't do well with the reality that it may be happening within a half-mile proximity of where I am at the moment. As I said before, I'm not one of these people who throw up if you throw up around me, I just despise throw-uppers for a really long time when it's done within my presence. I hold a vomit grudge against the violator of my phobia. And I didn't want to be forced to treat Luke harshly because of his ailment. To see Luke walking to my truck with a trash can wasn't good. I knew it wasn't, because this trash can matched his outfit.

The entire drive to the ER, I was laboring before the Lord in prayer:

God, don't let him throw up in this car. I'll sin no more. I'll give my savings away. I'll fast for forty days. Help me, dear Lord, help me!

Thankfully, it wasn't until I had dropped him off and was parking my truck that he lost his cookies.

His wife worked at the hospital as a nurse, so the three of us waited for a little while in a small room for a doctor to come check him out.

The doctor arrived and began asking questions, and Luke was being quite vague. So I jumped in and said, "Doctor, yesterday in the gym, the dude did push-ups while hanging a seventy-five-pound dumbbell around his neck. That's what happened." His wife, Lindsay, was embarrassed. The doctor wasn't amused.

"You hung a seventy-five-pound dumbbell around your neck?"

"Yes sir."

"And you're getting a master's degree?"

"Yes sir."

"You know that your body was created to do certain things, right?"

"Yes sir."

"And your body was not created to do certain things. Your body was not created to hang seventy-five-pound weights from your neck. It goes against how our bodies were made to function."

Luke would be fine. He had a minor injury, and he fully recovered. Yet that statement from the doctor stuck with both of us:

Your body was not created to do certain things . . . it goes against how our bodies were made to function.

And so it is with the church.

The church is often referred to as "the body of Christ." And this body—the church—was created to do certain things and to be aligned correctly to the heart, mission, and purposes of God. To function in ways we weren't created to function leads to being sidetracked, distracted, and removed from our purpose.

This happens when we focus more on perfecting the Sunday morning worship hour than on equipping people to live for God throughout the week.

This happens when we worship *worship* more than we worship God.

This happens when we choose safety over engagement.

This happens when we're known more for what we are against than what we are for.

This happens when we ignore the pain of Latinos, African Americans, the LGBTQ community, the poor, and injustices in our cities.

This happens when we give in to fear, instead of being driven by radical trust.

This happens when we resort to talking about others, instead of talking to others.

Jesus Had a Neutral Gear

Back to the Jesus Paradigm in Luke 6. After spending the night in prayer with God, Jesus came down from the mountain and immediately called together twelve disciples who would become known as the twelve apostles. It would be Jesus's primary community, close friends, and support system. Though Jesus wouldn't give them any commands or tasks until Luke 9 (three chapters later), you read about the twelve being present in most of the stories. Their task was to watch Jesus, study Jesus, learn from Jesus, and follow Jesus.

From solitude, Jesus rallied together a close-knit community, because the heart of God, since Genesis 1–2, was to invite humans to partner with him to live life, and to care for God's world.

Think about it: Jesus, the Son of God, was in need of meaningful relationships . . . a tight-knit community. And if he was in need of it, how much more are we?

The vitality of solitude and the need for community are meant to mesh, interlock, and dance. Together they form rhythm that sets the heart and body into motion with God.

In the book of Acts, what shocks me about Acts 2 isn't just that three thousand were saved in one day, but it is what the three thousand people began to do. They didn't just respond to a moment or an event; they gave in to a new kind of life. Acts 2:42 tells us that they devoted themselves to prayer, growth, mission, and community. Solo missions are rare in God's kingdom. Jesus believed in doing ministry in community, which is why he often sent people out in pairs. Through community, kingdom witness shines the brightest.

Pet the Dog

I've heard few people talk more about the need for meaningful community than Buddy Bell. He told a story once about a family who left their dog at a doggy motel while they went on vacation for a week. Upon returning from their trip, they picked their dog up, but they didn't understand why their dog was shedding hair over the next few hours. Their dog didn't shed, yet hair was falling out everywhere.

So they called the veterinarian, thinking their dog might have a virus. The vet told them to simply pet the dog. The dog had been away from the touch of its family, and it was simply in need of its family's touch. They began petting the dog, and sure enough, hair quit falling out.

The moral of that story is that the next time you see a bald person at church or out in public, go up and pet them like a dog, and maybe hair will grow back. Just don't tell them I told you to do it, cool?

In Jesus's kingdom, *a meaningful touch* may not mean a physical touch, but it is a connection that takes place between two or more people for the sake of encouragement, edification, and reconciliation. It's important to realize that Jesus-followers are not called to be acquaintances, nor are they called to be best friends with everyone. Yet there is a calling to live into a tight-knit community where spiritual formation, growth, maturity, and mission are viable possibilities and expectations.

Jesus didn't call twelve people who were clones of one another. In that little group, there were fishermen, tax collectors, a betrayer, and a zealot. These were all Jews, yet they came into this Jesus community with different experiences, motives, and convictions. And Jesus brought them together into what would become the greatest force the world has ever known: *the church*.

We have no clue if the twelve apostles had much of a relationship before Jesus called them. We don't know if they were friends, neighbors, or if they even had respect for one another. We don't know if they had ever served together, partnered in a project, or if they sat next to each other in the youth group.

Jesus didn't call together twelve people who had already formed tight bonds and were on board with the same mission and vision in life. We assume they were from the same area, and we know they were all Jews, but we don't know if they came from the same neighborhood.

We do know they differed politically, socio-economically, and in how they thought the Jews should cooperate (or not cooperate) with the powers of the world.

Jesus didn't call people who already loved each other into community. He called people into community and taught them to love each other.

Our tendency is to gravitate toward people who look like us, live like us, smell like us, dress like us, and vote like us. It makes for quick connections, similar hobbies, and familiar environments. Yet the Jesus way is more risky than that. It's more inclusive. It's more dangerous.

A few weeks ago, someone told me the story of a school in the Dallas/Fort Worth area which has a special program for those who are significantly visually impaired. In preparation for the parent/teacher night, the teacher had an eye doctor create glasses for the parents to wear that would give them an idea of what it was like to see (or not to see) the world the way their children did. As the parents put the glasses on, tears began to flow. Seeing the world through the lens of their children opened them up to a new reality.

In Acts 9, when Saul was converted, God went straight for his eyes. In fact, we read that when Saul was baptized, something like scales fell from his eyes. For the sake of the assignment God was giving Saul (whose name would change to Paul), God had to change the way Saul *saw* the world. Specifically, God had to change the way Saul *saw* people. He was a racist. He had been swallowed up by nationalistic fervor for the Jewish race. God had to reset his eyes.

Meaningful community only happens when we allow ourselves to see others the way God sees them. Too often the lenses we prefer to wear are tainted, blurry, and fuzzy because of personal bias.

Have you noticed how easy it is to project certain labels on people before we take the time to know them?

For example, when I see a car with a Roll Tide bumper sticker, my first thought is, *Arrogant*. (And let's be honest, love or hate the Tide, they have reason to be, right?)

When you're walking through a store and you see someone with a "Stronger Together" or "Make America Great Again" shirt on, you already begin thinking certain things about that person.

Over the last couple of years, we have seen the rise of the Black Lives Matter (BLM) movement. When some hear those three letters, they think justice, liberation, and human rights. Others hear them and immediately think about protests, riots, and shutting down bridges. I've been invited into meetings with some of the most influential African American leaders and pastors in Memphis. Though I'm constantly discerning how to be a voice for those who don't have a voice, what I gain the most from is hearing the questions and issues that are driving people.

The place to be educated about the current state of many of the African Americans in our country isn't by reading Facebook posts or by sitting around a table with five white people discussing black culture. It is by sitting with a person of color, asking open-ended questions and listening. And after you have listened, listen some more.

The reason I refuse to use #AllLivesMatter instead of #Black LivesMatter isn't because I don't believe that all lives matter equally to God. I believe this to the core. Every single person has been created by God, and God is eager for all people to come into a life-changing relationship with Jesus. I can unapologetically say #BlackLivesMatter, not because I believe they matter more than others, but because I believe they matter just as much as others.

When God told Jonah to go preach to the Ninevites, Jonah was reluctant. He didn't want to go.

Go to the Ninevites.

Nah, I don't want to.

I need you to go, because they need to know that they matter.

Nope. All lives matter, right?

Yes, all lives matter. But today, the Ninevites need to know how much they matter!

When Jesus engaged a Samaritan woman in John 4, his disciples were stunned. Why would Jesus break social barriers and religious code like this?

It wasn't the time for Jesus to teach the disciples how much all lives matter to God. It was a moment for them to see that there are times when the face of God turns toward a specific person or race to let them know how much they matter to God.

Choosing to exist, invest, and enter meaningful community takes great humility, and the willingness to understand the other . . . whoever the other may be. Arrogance doesn't play well in our world, and rarely does it lead to a good end. Not only does it slowly rot the soul, it is also a primary tool in the hands of the enemy to destroy community.

Diversity is a present-day gift, because it is also our future reality. And though it makes community more difficult, it also makes community stronger.

Recently my family attended an event, and it just so happened that it was full of white people. There's nothing inherently bad about this. Yet my seven-year-old noticed.

"Hey, did you notice there aren't any dark-skinned people here?"

"Well, yes, I guess I did."

"I like when black people and white people are together . . . like at church and in Memphis."

Acknowledging Our Challenges

As I finish this chapter, Donald Trump has just been elected president. It was another polarizing election season. Verbal missiles were shot all over the place. Candidates resorted to negative ads and cutthroat campaign strategies. Unfortunately, many Christians blew their witness by social media behavior. I had one friend tweet: *A new believer grew up in Islam. It took believers in the flesh to help him overcome the hurdle of "believers" on social media.*

Months ago, as I looked at the political, spiritual, and cultural climate around us, I would have used the word *wedge* to describe the distance between the church and culture, or even churches and other churches. Yet, post-election, I realize it isn't a wedge, but a huge chasm. And do we care? Does the church care?

Reality is this:

Eighty-one percent of white evangelicals voted for Trump.

Eighty-eight percent of blacks voted for Clinton.

Only 37 percent of millennials voted for Trump; 55 percent voted for Clinton.

And 26 percent of religious unaffiliated voted Trump. Which means the large majority of them did not.

When there is resistance between people, a race, a group . . . one can choose to press against and to push away, or to step into the mess of conflict to reach for the other. One can turn away or turn toward.

Jesus called together a diverse community and told them that the way they loved each other would be both a witness and an invitation to the world of the love of God that can fill a community. And then Jesus taught this community how to stand on convictions, while not forsaking the mission of engaging the world. In God's kingdom, convictions don't exempt people from risky living. Instead, they fuel it.

Learning from Norway

Back to Rjukan.

When they created their cable car, they provided a way for people to be carried toward the light. However, a few years ago, there were a few people who decided that wasn't enough. Some artists and inventors decided to do something about it. In 1913, it was first suggested that they should add mirrors to reflect the sun. And a few people nearly a century later decided to make that a reality.

The idea was to bring in three huge mirrors, with the intent to reflect the sun into the town. However, there was one problem: the mirrors were going to be expensive ... to the tune of a million dollars. This was going to cost the taxpayers.

Immediately, they faced opposition. Petitions and letter-writing campaigns circulated, and Facebook pages to halt progress were created and shared. Concerned citizens argued that the money should be spent on schools, roads, to create jobs, and other efforts in the city.

The mirrors went up. And when they did, many gathered in the town square to experience it. They were told that the reflection of the sun would only shine into a small area, but that didn't keep people from bringing beach chairs and sunglasses, and pouring margaritas with little umbrellas.

The sun reflected into the town, and smiles came across faces. As the objectors saw the faces of people light up, some of their hearts softened. Robert Jenbergsen said, "I thought it would be a waste because we have a lot of bad weather here, but when we got the sun, you could see the happiness it brought. We had never seen anything like that before. So, now I think it is great." [3]

Visitors and tourists increased, and a hi-tech company relocated to Rjukan. The mirrors brought light and life.

Sometimes the church is called to carry people to the light, and sometimes we are called to reflect it into the shadows. Our ultimate call of God is not to be spectacular or famous, but to simply be faithful to how God is drawing people to himself. Jesus called together a community and injected them with light, and the church is called to do the same.

Notes

[1]Jon Henley, "Rjukan Sun: the Norwegian Town That Does It with Mirrors," *Guardian*, November 6, 2013, https://www.theguardian.com/world/2013/nov/06/rjukan-sun-norway-town-mirrors.

[2]Luke Norsworthy has a popular podcast. You should check it out: *Newsworthy with Norsworthy*, at lukenorsworthy.com.

[3]Suzanne Daley, "Beaming Good Cheer to a Norwegian Town's Dark Days," *New York Times*, April 13, 2014, https://www.nytimes.com/2014/04/14/world/europe/beaming-good-cheer-to-a-norwegian-towns-dark-days.html?_r=0.

CHAPTER 11

Reimagining Justice

While I was in college, my good friend Sarah Campbell and
I were hired to be the cointerim youth ministers at the Highland
Church in Abilene. It was 2001, and the events of 9/11 happened
during our second week on the job. We found ourselves sitting
in a room with dozens of teenagers attempting to process faith,
suffering, tragedy, evil, and the movement of God.

In the months that followed, we spent most of our time calling
people into the heart of a God we claim to be good. We focused
on prayer, Bible study, worship, adoration, gratitude, silence, surrender, and other ways that connect our hearts to his.

Come November, though, we realized we had done a lot of
"personal relationship with God" stuff, but we hadn't called our
students into the world. We hadn't talked to them much about
compassion, justice, service, and risk. We wanted to have a more
holistic approach to spirituality. So we decided to do something
about that.

We had heard of a social club at ACU (Gata) that had an activity in which they took an evening to call their members to do
random acts of kindness throughout Abilene. And we decided to

do something similar. We called the event "Give It Up." Each kid was encouraged to bring fifteen dollars. Of these funds, five dollars would go to a pizza party and the other ten dollars would go into a pot. We gathered on a Sunday evening, split them up into groups of three to five, and gave them about thirty minutes to think of what they would do if they had one hour to do "random acts of kindness in the name of Jesus" throughout the city of Abilene. After thirty minutes, we gave each group around sixty dollars and told them to be back in an hour.

I stayed behind to set up the room for dinner and to wait on the pizza. The plan was for everyone to come back, eat pizza, and share stories about the adventure. I also had to go get cups and some ice. However, I wanted a story to tell about taking a risk too, so I took a few extra dollars with me to the grocery store.

It took a little longer than I thought, and I was running out of time, so as I paid, I handed the woman at the checkout an extra fifteen dollars and said, "Ma'am, will you do something for me? I'm part of a group right now that is attempting to spread love and kindness through Abilene. Whoever comes up behind me, will you pay for whatever they have and tell them that this is done in the name of Jesus?"

She looked at me with this blank stare.

I repeated myself, "Ma'am, I know this sounds bizarre, but please, take this fifteen dollars, and whoever comes next, pay for whatever they have, and please tell them that this has been done for them in the name of Jesus."

She agreed.

I reached the glass doors to walk into the parking lot, and curiosity came over me. I wondered if anyone was walking up yet, and if so, who they might be and what this small act of love might do for them. I was surprised when I saw two men walk up to the counter carrying nothing but a six-pack of beer. And I stood and watched the cashier shrug her shoulders, hold up the fifteen dollars, and tell them that their beer was being paid for in the name of Jesus.

So, yes, I was a twenty-one-year-old minister who bought beer for someone in the name of Jesus.

Everyone returned to the church with smiles on their faces. As we sat to eat pizza, we began sharing stories. I went first, and we all got a good laugh out of it. And then the students began to share.

One group went through the drive-through at fast-food restaurants and paid for the cars behind them along with notes about how much Jesus loved them.

Another bought roses and delivered them to nurses at the hospital.

We had a group buy stuffed animals to give to children in the hospital.

Another bought a bike for a child in a community whose family couldn't afford one.

After one group purchased huge tubs of ice cream, they went to the porch of a single mother with four kids, and together they had a dozen plastic spoons digging into "cookies and cream" while they shared stories together.

One thing I heard from so many people that night was this, "What we did tonight really isn't that hard." And they were right. Some of God's best work through us doesn't come from flowcharts, planned events, or even well-thought-out strategies. It comes from choosing to embrace Jesus's rhythm as our own; and from conviction, kingdom work happens.

Following Jesus Wherever He Goes

Mother Teresa is often attributed with saying, "Do small things with great love." But it was Jesus who first lived it, and he lived it to the fullest.

After spending the night in solitude and prayer, Jesus descended from the mountain and called together his twelve apostles. Jesus moved from solitude to community. Yet, Jesus both taught and lived that a life with God isn't solely based on prayer time and friendship. Quiet time with God and social time with friends don't necessarily lead to the godly life. It is incomplete. It is missing a vital component, because God's heart isn't set to the tune of absorbing prayers and cultivating fellowship.

In Luke 6, Jesus moves from solitude, to community, to ministry and service.

> He came down with them and stood on a level place,
> with a great crowd of his disciples and a great multitude
> of people from all Judea, Jerusalem, and the coast of
> Tyre and Sidon. They had come to hear him and to be
> healed of their diseases; and those who were troubled
> with unclean spirits were cured. And all in the crowd
> were trying to touch him, for power came out from him
> and healed all of them. Then he looked up at his disci-
> ples and said: "Blessed are you who are poor . . ."
> (Luke 6:17–20)

The Jesus Rhythm involves the head, heart, and hands. It is solitude, community, and compassion. It's the rhythm you see throughout the rest of Jesus's public ministry, and not only that, it is also the rhythm of the church in Acts. It's not always solitude that leads to community, and then community that leads to compassion. Don't think of it as a direct progression, but three components that weave together.

Jesus's ministry in Luke 6 included healing, driving out demons, and teaching. It was a ministry of liberation, authority, demonstration of God's power, and proclamation. It was actions and words.

I'm not arguing that the call of God is for your life and rhythm—and the church's life and rhythm—to be a third solitude, a third community, and a third ministry and service. Yet I think honoring these commitments helps to form a well-rounded follower of Jesus.

∿

The people I met with in Barrow didn't use language or paradigms of solitude, community, and ministry, but there were consistent echoes of them. The themes of faith, friendship, and service were noticeable threads.

Barrow is a whaling community. In fact, the whale is their mascot. They are the Whalers. Few people have more respect in the Barrow community than those who lead the whaling expeditions. Though only a few go out hunting for them, the community comes together to celebrate. Though there are many laws now that protect certain species, it is recognized that whaling is deeply woven into the DNA of their culture. Hauling a whale to shore is no joke. It's quite a task. And once it arrives, they throw parties, because the entire community benefits.

The meat is called *muktuk*, and the natives love it. Kyle and I were talking to a guy one day about *muktuk*, and he attempted to describe the taste. We were interested in trying some until he said that it tastes like frozen bubblegum. *Frozen bubblegum?* After that, we decided to pass.

Bringing in a whale takes energy, sacrifice, time, and great effort. Yet, the community benefits from it.

It's difficult to live in a place with the weather conditions of Barrow without relying on the community. You need each other; not just for social awareness, but for survival. You serve one another, because life may depend on it.

In places throughout the world where living conditions are strenuous (for whatever reason), trust is as vital to the community as an organ is to the body. However, for a new person coming into the community, trust is not easily given. It must be earned.

In Barrow, the median family income is just shy of $100,000. Therefore, there is an attraction to the area. In fact, one person shared with me that 90 percent of the teachers at the local high school were actually from the lower forty-eight states. They come to Barrow during the school year and leave in the summer. They may work in Barrow for a few years, but they don't see it as a permanent place to call home. For the indigenous folks in the area, or even for those who've lived there for a lengthy period of time, this becomes an integrity issue. It's hard for the community to trust someone who isn't showing that they are willing to invest in the community.

And I get it. Don't you?

Christianity in Culture

One reason many people in our current culture struggle to trust the church is because the church doesn't have a viable presence in the culture. The church may show up to pass out flyers for their Easter or Halloween event, and then to pass out turkeys, but their absence is often noticeable and even felt. One of the best things we can do to impact the world is this: *show up*.

An image the Bible uses to describe your spiritual act of worship is to be "a living sacrifice."

Think about it: a *living sacrifice*? Isn't that an oxymoron like jumbo shrimp or organized government? How could you be a *living sacrifice*? Sacrifices don't live. A lamb never returned to his flock to tell them about his appointment at the sacrifice earlier in the day.

Sacrifices don't live. They die.

But not with Jesus.

Sacrifices are now poured out *before* God and *for* others. In Jesus, sacrifices are not where we die, but where we spread life. Sacrifices live, move, walk, and go.

Ask yourself, who am I pouring my life out for?

How Anointing Works

For the first few years in our Memphis community known as Binghampton, we lived in two smaller homes. The first one was a rental and was roughly 850 square feet, and the second, which we bought, was a little over 900. Both were two-bedroom, one-bath homes.

When we bought our home, we knew we needed to completely renovate the kitchen, so we did. However, it took over seven weeks to do it. So, for seven weeks our 900-square-foot home became a 600-square-foot home as we lived without a kitchen, dining room, and washer and dryer. Oh, and our boys were ages five and three at the time.

We can look back and laugh now, but living through it was a nightmare. A friend let us borrow a tiny refrigerator to store milk and a few things, but other than that, a toaster and outside grill were our only ways to cook. We did the best we could. We ate on paper plates as much as possible, because the only place to wash dishes was in the bathtub. We discovered that children eat free on Mondays and Tuesdays at Central BBQ, and at Moe's near the University of Memphis campus on Thursdays. Those two restaurants became our frequent hangouts.

To make it even more of a challenge, our three-year-old, Noah, decided he was ready to begin potty training. Again, we had no washer and dryer, which meant we either had to clean his messes in the bathtub, or simply throw clothes away.

A few years later, we decided to completely remodel our only bathroom. It was pretty bad. There was mold around the edges, 1950 tile on the walls, a hole in the door, and when you sat on the toilet, your knees would hit the bathtub. To say it was in poor condition is an understatement. But more than anything, it was somewhat embarrassing when company came over. The door wouldn't lock, and we had to often apologize when people came out because you could hear knees hitting the plastic bathtub.

Kayci is far from being dramatic, needy, and high maintenance. She loves the simple life. But I can recall a few occasions when she would walk out of the bathroom with tears in her eyes, and it wasn't because she had eaten too much chili. It's because the bathroom was in poor condition, and she shared it with two small boys who had (and still have) awful aim.

When we decided to gut and remodel the bathroom, Kayci said we needed to find somewhere to live for two weeks. I wasn't so sure. I argued for wet wipes in the place of showers, but she wasn't buying. She asked where we would use the restroom, and I told her that the boys and I could use the backyard and she could go to the closest Kroger's or Walgreens. My idea didn't go over very well. We stayed with friends for a few days.

It wasn't that Kayci was desperate for more space, for we have learned so much about God through living simpler, more simplistic lives. It was that the space was squeezing her, and us.

She used words like *pressed*, *squeezed*, and *crammed*.

Have you ever felt pressed by life, squeezed by circumstances, suffocated by stress, or crammed because of busyness?

If you have, I bet you felt exhausted.

However, there are times when being pressed and squeezed is what blesses the world. Let me explain.

The word *anoint* shows up a few times throughout the Bible. Multiple times Jesus had women anoint him with oil. In the book of James, the sick are encouraged to have the elders anoint them with oil. The name *Christ* also means "the anointed one." And in 1 John 2:27, we read, "As for you, the *anointing* that you received from him abides in you, and so you do not need anyone to teach you. But as his *anointing* teaches you about all things, and is true and is not a lie, and just as it has taught you, abide in him" (emphasis added).

I didn't grow up in a faith tradition that used the word *anointing* much. It wasn't in our vocabulary. We were a tradition that didn't know what to do with the Holy Spirit. It wasn't taught this way, but there was this underlying idea that the Holy Spirit's best days were in the book of Acts. For a couple of decades, the Spirit was on Red Bull and steroids. He had energy, adrenaline, and miraculous power. However, once the apostles died, it's as if the Holy Spirit took some NyQuil, and has been on cruise control ever since.

Thankfully, God has expanded my appreciation for the work of the Spirit in my life, in the church, and in the world. One of the functions of the Holy Spirit—and there are a few—is that the Spirit plays a major role in what it means to be anointed by God.

When it came to Jesus being anointed by women (Matt. 26:6–7, Luke 7:38), or James commanding the sick to be anointed by oil (James 5:14), it's important to know there was a process in making and preparing oil.

Olive oil was used for cooking, soap, lighting candles, and even as medicine. It should go without saying that it was a valuable resource for everyday life. However, you didn't walk up to an olive tree and walk away with oil. It involved a lengthier process.

Once removed from the tree, olives were taken to an olive press, where they would be pressed and squeezed. The olive press was a huge stone block, and once the olives were pressed, oil would flow.

Without the pressing, there would be no oil.

If the olives were not squeezed and crushed, nothing would flow.

And if oil didn't flow, anointings wouldn't happen.

For humanity and for the entire world, anointing doesn't flow from God's heart the way it does if someone isn't pressed, squeezed, and crushed. The night before Jesus was crucified, we are told he prayed at the Mount of Olives. I wonder how close he was to an olive press. To glance at a press, and to envision the cross that was set before him, he knew that the pain would be great, yet the anointing that would flow would be an unleashed, untapped power the world had never seen before and would never see again.

Anointing flows because something—or someone—has been pressed.

Without sacrifice, anointing doesn't flow.

There is an anointing of God's mercy, compassion, love, and joy, and for some reason, God intends for it to flow through his people. It only happens when we step with God into adventure, sacrifice, risk, and faith.

There is a place in a Christian's life for solitude and meaningful fellowship, but if we fail to move into arenas where compassion needs to flow, we stunt our own spiritual development, and we hinder the advancement of the kingdom around us. Prayer closets and close social groups are necessary, but with no extension of God's grace and compassion, we become inactive. Compassion becomes a check we write or an annual gift we give.

The rhythm of Jesus included the sick, broken, and those held in bondage. Jesus stepped into their mess, and so should those who call him Lord. Said differently, we can step into the mess of others because Jesus was willing to step into ours.

Learning from Ground Zero

In 2006, my good friend Josh Graves told me about St. Paul's Chapel in Manhattan. At the time, I had never been to New York City, and I had never heard of St. Paul's Chapel. That would change in 2008. Our worship minister, Kip Long, and I traveled to New York City to attend a Tuesday-night prayer meeting at the Brooklyn Tabernacle, and when we did, we spent some time at St. Paul's Chapel. Since then, I've been to New York City four times, and each time I have spent time at the chapel that stands across the street from where the towers fell.

Built in the 1760s, it is the longest-standing building in Manhattan. President Washington, other presidents, and members of Congress have worshipped there. In fact, when you visit today, you will see the pew George Washington used to call his own. For those of you who have been sitting in the same seat for decades, don't get any ideas. Your pew is not going to be retired one day.

Not only has this church survived wear and tear, weather and decay, it has survived the Great New York City Fire of 1776, as well as the crumbling of the towers, which fell across the street. Not even a window was broken.

As rescue crews began sifting through rubble for survivors and bodies, a request was made for St Paul's Chapel to become a safe haven for workers and volunteers. Their doors would remain open for months, 24/7, serving people. It became a physical and spiritual hospital. Workers would come into the chapel for nourishment, therapy, rest, and rejuvenation. The sanctuary was sacred space. It provided food, drinks, massage therapists, music, and healing. Even President George Washington's retired pew was used. Nothing was off limits.

However, if you came into St. Paul's Chapel for healing, nourishment, and therapy, there was an expectation that you were resting up to go right back into the grind. You entered sacred space knowing you were being equipped to leave the same space because you were on a mission.

It's a remarkable image of what it means for the church to be the church. Church is not just the place we go to meet with God, but it is where we learn how to meet God everywhere else. The church gathers, and the church scatters.

The local church cannot afford to sit around asking questions about who our target audience needs to be. Instead, we need to step outside our facilities, or drive around our neighborhoods, and claim whatever it is we see as the harvest that is plentiful.

Moving forward into the twenty-first century, the church—the people of God—cannot afford to sit back in our worship assemblies and think that is the primary function God requires. We must enter—and reenter—into the heart of God's mission.

God is inviting us into the world to be a part of how he is redeeming the world. It's time for us to march.

PART 4

Christmas Trees and Fruit Trees

I can count on one hand how many times I've been hiking. I'm a city boy. It probably doesn't help that the places I've called home aren't known for their hiking experiences. When I have hiked, it has been with people who love to do so. It is a good thing for me, because they know what they are doing. One thing I have noticed is that when I'm on an adventure with experienced hikers, they often take moments to pause, get their bearings, take a sip of water, remind themselves where we are going, and then plot out the path that will get us there.

On the journey of life, there will be moments and seasons that hit with paralyzing force. The fork in the road, and the decisions we make, may not be heaven-or-hell decisions, but status quo vs. joy, mediocrity vs. hope, being defined by the past vs. pressing into the future. Some of the healthiest and best questions we need to be prepared to ask in life are:

Where do I go from here?

What now?

With my current pace and rhythm in life, what am I becoming?

How does God want me to move forward from this place?

❧

When I left Barrow, there was sadness. Sure, I was missing my wife and kids like crazy, but I didn't feel like Barrow's people and culture were finished with me. I also knew the chances of me ever returning were slim. You don't accidentally end up in Barrow, Alaska. In eleven days, the small town had taught me valuable lessons about life, but I left knowing there was so much more Barrow had to give.

My prayer became, "God, for all this trip has taught me about light, darkness, roots, rhythm, and about you, let it have its way with me. Help me to reflect faithfully. Help me know what to do with this experience."

One way to think about what we are becoming is to think about the Christmas tree and the fruit tree.

Growing up, we had a family tradition of picking out our Christmas tree at a farm. It was quite the experience. Around Thanksgiving, we would pile into our blue Astro van, travel to a Christmas tree farm, cut down our tree of choice, tie it to the top of the van, and travel back home. Once in the house, we had to put it in its stand, where it would sit for the next few weeks. As kids, we complained about the entire experience. We didn't mind the tree; we loved Christmas! But getting in a van, picking out a tree, getting back in the van—it just didn't sit well with us as kids. It was boring.

Things changed when all three of us became teenagers. My mom decided to go with a fake tree instead. This cut out the tradition of picking out a tree. And all of a sudden, the three kids felt betrayed. Sure, we used to complain, but how dare our parents make a decision that ripped our Christmas tree tradition—complaining and all—right out from under our feet.

Whether the tree was real or fake, the tradition of decorating the tree lived on. My wife still does this today with our boys. Christmas music plays, hot chocolate is poured, Christmas candy is set out, and everyone begins to place lights, ornaments, and objects on the tree. Some ornaments don't have any meaning whatsoever, but most do. Some are pictures of Truitt and Noah when they were babies. There are ornaments with pictures of loved ones who are no longer with us. A few have Scripture references, or the names of Jesus written on them.

My grandmother had so much stuff that went on her tree, that instead of simplifying the number of ornaments and decorations, she chose to buy another tree instead. Then she proceeded to fill that one with creative wonder as well.

One year, my mom made gingerbread cookie ornaments, and she used Red Hots as the buttons of the coat. We came home from church one night to discover that our dog, Rufus, had eaten every ornament, but somehow managed to spit every single Red Hot into one pile with perfect precision.

Chances are we could find out quite a bit about a family based on what they hang on their Christmas tree. It tells you something about their values and convictions.

Fruit trees are quite different from Christmas trees. Many of us walk into grocery stores expecting to have fresh fruit every day of the year, and when the bananas are green or the peaches are too hard, we don't understand why. We feel like someone isn't doing their job. A lot of hard work goes into having fresh fruit in a supermarket. A tree has to be planted. It has to be properly nourished so it can grow. There is a harvest.

I'm not suggesting that fruit trees are better than Christmas trees, because some will immediately call me a Scrooge. But for the sake of this book—*and for the sake of the gospel*—I do think it is important to ask:

Do I want to be a Christmas tree or a fruit tree?

More importantly:

Does God want me to be like a Christmas tree or a fruit tree?

And one more question:

Are we raising our children to be Christmas trees or fruit trees?

Think about it. Christmas trees stay in the house. They do not leave the home. They are seasonal, and we hang stuff on them. They are for decoration.

Fruit trees are outside. For them to function properly, the nourishment they receive is not for themselves alone, but so they can offer what they have to others. The tree may never know where the fruit goes once it leaves. It simply trusts that the fruit it bears goes to bless the world.

Which are we becoming? Which are we raising the next generation to be?

∾

To engage in reentry, to cultivate healthy roots and rhythm, is first and foremost a gift from God. Just as he doesn't hoard his good gifts, he also doesn't withhold his invitation. It is God saying that anything he redeems is redeemed for a purpose. And I can't imagine our God frowning on any child of his who comes to him with a desire to live a more meaningful, adventurous life. There is a lot God can do with a willing, available, seeking heart.

My trip to Barrow wasn't simply about a getaway, a sermon series, or so I could have adventure stories to tell. It was a chance for me to learn from a culture about what it means to survive and thrive in life no matter what harsh elements press in on us. A core value in their culture is that thriving is not something individuals do on their own. They thrive together, for the sake of the community. Christ-followers should be able to understand that core value. God is interested in more than simply status change. He desires to set ablaze a community for the sake of his mission to redeem and restore the entire world.

No matter what season of darkness we are moving through or out of, the good news of Jesus invites us into a better place.

The good news of reentry is that it is for you.

The good news of reentry is that it is also for the world.

God restores the world through redeemed people.

And God restores people for the sake of redeeming the entire world.

CHAPTER 12

Reentry Matters for You

In the summer of 2015, I traveled to Colorado Springs for a couple of meetings. While there, I was invited to Mac and Mary Owen's home for dinner. Though I have only been around Mac and Mary a few times, I crave being with them, because they aren't just people who talk about freedom—they truly live it.

Mac is the national director of Celebrate Recovery, and Mary is the national training coach. Celebrate Recovery is now in over thirty thousand churches around the world, so the impact the Owens have is immeasurable. Basically, they travel the country encouraging and equipping leaders in CR. They don't do this because they are simply book-smart in the subject of recovery (which they are), but because they have lived it. They tell their story in their book *Never Let Go*.[1] Drugs, alcohol, codependency, sex out of marriage, child out of wedlock . . . their past includes decisions that could hinder progress because of their potential to bring guilt and shame, yet they have chosen to wake up each day declaring God's victory over their past, present, and future.

They live in the middle of nowhere. In fact, the directions were to drive forty-five minutes outside of Colorado Springs, turn at the Starbucks, drive a few more miles until you come to a dirt road, continue on that for a few more miles, and then turn into the driveway.

Driving there, I felt like I was in a horror movie. I'm a city boy. I don't do well on mountains or in the middle of a forest. I need to hear some planes, trains, sirens, or at least the sound of semitrucks on the interstate. On the way to their home, it was just woods, deer, elk, and more of the same.

They welcomed me into their home as if I was their own family. I shared with them about this book project, and we sat on their patio sharing stories about reentry and God's desire to lead people out of every form of darkness. At one point, Mary reminded me that the reason Jesus healed people wasn't just to keep them from dying, but to give them a chance to reenter the fabric of life.

Mac served at White's Ferry Road Church of Christ in Louisiana before moving to Colorado. It was there that they helped launch what is still one of the most vibrant Celebrate Recovery ministries in the world. It wasn't easy, though. When church becomes a safe place for the broken, things can get really messy. And let's be honest, too many church people prefer clean over messy. Mac told me that an elder at the church in Louisiana once said, "When the drug addicts got here, they taught the rest of us to be honest."

One thing I was interested in was how Mac and Mary establish roots and maintain a healthy rhythm in their lives. Their spiritual disciplines are strong. They trust their disciplines. In fact, they drove me around their land and took me to the places where they sit with God to reflect, breathe, and pour out their hearts to the Lord. In the shade, and surrounded by mountains, the Owens find rest in God. And thousands of people receive the benefits from their commitment to that resting place. Only God knows.

They lean on the very practices that keep them rooted in the heart of God, because they know if their disciplines fade and weaken, they become vulnerable and the power of their witness shrinks.

When it comes to roots, one thing I have discovered in my very limited experience in flower beds is that the season of greatest growth for flowers, trees, and grass is also the time when you have to fight the hardest against weeds. The times of greatest growth are also the times when you have to work against the weeds the most.

We live in a time when people struggle to commit to anything. Sure, we have short-term commitments, but as for long-term investment in relationships, jobs, neighborhoods, and the church, we waver and move on too quickly. We live in a time when it is extremely difficult to establish roots, because we don't give roots the time to develop. And uncultivated roots lead to unhealthy rhythm. It's just how it works.

Throughout this book I've shared how entry and reentry orient us into the heart of God, and into more meaningful lives. Without hearing and responding to the ongoing invitation of Jesus, we begin to settle in life. When we settle, we stagnate. When we stagnate, we cease to grow. And when we cease to grow, we no longer bear fruit.

I have a friend who pastors a church in the Midwest. Recently, he had a gifted associate pastor at his church get caught up in an emotional affair. There is no such thing as secret sin that doesn't have an impact on everyone else around us. When leaders get wrapped up in intentional sin, the entire church feels the impact. After a long journey, the associate pastor resigned. I was on the phone with my friend the night before it was announced to the church, and he said, "Josh, he is one of the most gifted musicians and pastors I've ever known. However, he didn't allow his character to keep pace with his giftedness."

He didn't allow his character to keep pace with his giftedness.

Unfortunately, I've witnessed the impact of this statement, and the profound effect it has on individuals, communities, churches, and even a nation. When gifted people focus on their gift and not on their character, destruction is nearby.

But the good news is that even for those who have given in to severe character flaws and moral failures, life isn't over. Remember, God's track record of calling sinful people with dark pasts and broken people back into his heart and mission is long, and still growing.

As we reenter into the fabric of God's plan and purpose for our lives, we often are faced with difficult decisions. Sometimes the decision is to replace a bad habit, or sin, with something more positive and life-giving. Yet there are other times when the decision is about where to work, where to live, whether to move or not, or what relationships can no longer go into the future with us.

To Start Over or to Remodel

I've only cried during a few shows or movies. Here they are:

- *The Fresh Prince of Bel-Air.* The final episode was in May 1996, and I felt like someone cut me open and stole my kidney.
- *Old Yeller.* Because who hasn't.
- *The Notebook.* I didn't cry once. I cried twice. Loud. In the theater. It was embarrassing.
- *Katy Perry: Part of Me.* Don't judge me. The scene where her marriage was in trouble tore me to pieces.
- Lastly, basically any Special Olympics commercial, video of soldiers coming home, or the inspirational pieces on *College GameDay.*

Only one other show has brought a tear to my eye a time or two: *Extreme Home Makeover.* It seems that every single time they yell, "Move that bus," something moves in my throat. I can't help it.

One thing I noticed in *Extreme Home Makeover* is that in nearly every episode, a decision had to be made. Were they going to remodel what was standing, or were they going to knock it down and start from scratch?

Restore what is broken? Or make it brand-new?

Which one does God prefer? Restoring what is broken, or making it brand-new?

The answer: both!

The Bible teaches too much about new creation to think that God only prefers to restore what has been broken, but the Bible speaks too much about restoring what is broken to think God only wants to make things new.

So, when it comes to you reentering into the light—reentering into the fabric of life—what do you need to move away from? What darkness is God inviting you out of? Is it time for you to start all over again? Or is it time for you to surrender a broken heart, broken dreams, or misplaced allegiances in order to be restored by God into something that reflects his character and nature?

The Grass Isn't Always Greener

In the days of Isaac—way back in Genesis 26—having a well was often your source of life. It provided water for nourishment, cooking, and animals, and so much more. Without a well, survival was at risk. With a well, a community could properly function.

If an enemy wanted to cripple a community, what they would do is fill up a well. That is exactly what happened in Genesis 26:15. "Now the Philistines had stopped up and filled with earth all the wells that his father's servants had dug in the days of his father Abraham."

The wells had been clogged up. So, now what are they to do?

In our lives today, we have compassion wells, prayer wells, justice wells, family wells, and many other wells that are vital to survival, health, and transformation. Satan's desire is to fill up our wells, for if they are clogged, they don't function correctly. What I have learned in my life is that most of the time, the powers of darkness do not prefer to use a dump truck to fill up our wells, but a small shovel. One scoop at a time. Slowly filling up our wells, in a way that we hardly notice; until one day we look and see that our well no longer looks right.

What would Isaac do, because the community needed a well to function? He could dig a brand-new one. Or he could attempt to redig the wells of his father. I think both options would have been pleasing to God, but Isaac chose to redig the well.

> Isaac dug again the wells of water that had been dug in the days of his father Abraham; for the Philistines had stopped them up after the death of Abraham; and he gave them the names that his father had given them. (Gen. 26:18)

Sometimes, we need a new start. We need to leave the past behind and forge a new way. This involves risk, adventure, sacrifice, and great faith. I'm all for you taking this course if you feel it is right for you, but I want you to make sure it is right. We are too quick to jump ship, quit one job for another, leave one relationship for another, leave this church for that, and make swift changes, thinking that the grass is always greener on the other side. Make sure the new start is of God.

Sometimes we need to redig where the blessings and promises have flowed in the past. This also involves risk, adventure, sacrifice, and great faith. The elements of pain, darkness, and regret may be close by as we dig again, but God is able to bring forth something new from what has been broken.

There is a prayer practice I often use to center me in God, and it has also become a practice I lead our church through a few times a year. It involves your physical posture, so it is good to make sure you are sitting upright, with nothing in your lap. You begin by putting your hands palms-down on your lap. This represents what it is you need to lay down at the throne of God. It can be anything. It can be sin, an unhealthy emotion, a relationship, a habit, etc. After sitting with God in this posture for a while, you turn your hands over, palms up. This represents a receiving posture. Take time to receive from the Lord. Ask God to dispense a gift, a word, a revelation, a blessing.

It is a practice that centers and orients. Give it a shot. See what God will do. I think you'll find it helpful for the process of reentry and reengagement.

Whatever your path is, I am rooting for you to live into your freedom.

Our God is for you.

His invitation goes on forever.

His gift of reentry remains.

And remember, this gift of reentry isn't for you alone; it is to share with the world.

Note

[1]Mac and Mary Owen, *Never Let Go* (Batavia, IL: Lucas Lane, 2013).

CHAPTER 13

Reentry Matters for the World

A few years ago, I was speaking at a church outside of Tampa, Florida. I was dropped off at the airport about thirty minutes before my flight was scheduled to leave, and I was thrilled to see that the security line wasn't very long. As I got to the front of the line to show the woman sitting on a stool my ID and ticket, everyone in front of me began pointing behind me. They weren't just pointing; some were pulling out their phones and taking pictures. I turned around to see the man himself . . . Hulk Hogan.

I rushed through security and hurried to my gate. They were about to shut the door when I arrived, and I was relieved when I got onto the tarmac to see that there was a line of people. I had made my flight.

That's when I could see out of my peripheral vision that Hulk Hogan was walking up behind me. This meant that we would be in line next to each other for a few minutes waiting to board our flight.

I told myself, "Don't freak out, bro! Act like you've been here before. Play it cool. Don't turn into a twelve-year-old."

My pep talk helped, because people in front of me took a different approach. They were taking pictures, waving, and even calling out in their deepest Hogan-impersonation voices, "Hey, brother!"

He had sunglasses on and stared at the ground as if to avoid eye contact with others. And that's when I decided to move in. My arms were crossed. We still hadn't made eye contact. I was staring straight ahead. I leaned back. And said, "Hey, dude, are these people taking pictures of you or me?"

Hogan began laughing at me. Seriously, people! Hogan thought I was funny. I couldn't care less if you all think I'm funny or not. Hulk Hogan laughed, and that's something I'm going to take to the grave with me.

He then proceeded to engage me in conversation.

"Where are you from, man?"

I didn't miss a beat, "Well, my wife and I lived in Texas the first twenty-seven years of our lives, but a few years ago we relocated to Memphis."

He said, "I bet I was wrestling in Memphis before you were born."

"I was born in 1980."

"I was wrestling in Memphis in 1978."

After making small talk about Memphis culture, Memphis food, and Memphis music, he said this, "I've got to ask, man. Why would someone who was born and raised in Texas move to a place like Memphis, Tennessee?"

He may have meant absolutely nothing by it, but I didn't really like the way he said it. You see, I get really defensive of people who want to bash Memphis. Kayci and I love this city, and we want other people to love it too. It's to the point that when people talk down on Memphis, some of my nonviolent tendencies begin to break down, and I need to step away from people because I want to take a swing or give a nice shove (in the name of Jesus, of course). But I decided to give Hogan some grace that day. And he better be glad I did!

I thought for a minute, and responded this way: "Well, when it comes down to it, my wife and I are followers of Jesus, and a few years ago we had an opportunity to move to Memphis. And we decided that we needed to run into the fight. Unfortunately, some people write off Memphis as a place that is corrupt, divided, and hopeless; but for us, that seemed like a place that the power of the resurrection may break out, and if so, we wanted to get in on it. We believe Memphis is a city worth fighting for."

Hogan pointed at me. And to be honest, when he did, I flinched. Have you seen his finger? That thing could have chopped my head off.

And he said, "That's cool, man. That's cool."

And that was the end of our conversation. I walked back to coach, and he went to the front of the plane.

Yet I sat down in my seat and began to think about what I had just told him. I told Hulk Hogan that I believe Memphis—my context—is worth fighting for. The rest of the flight, I reflected on that confession, and attempted to think through how it is evident in my life. I don't want to speak bold things with my mouth if my actions don't follow. I do not want to be a living contradiction.

Is Memphis a city worth fighting for, and how do my actions line up with that commitment?

How about you? Is your context worth fighting for, and how are the actions of your life lining up with that commitment? Invitations from God don't simply prepare us for eternity, but for his ongoing mission.

A Context Worth Fighting For

In the middle of the Lord's Prayer, Jesus taught us to pray, "Your kingdom come, your will be done, on earth as it is in heaven." Jesus doesn't pray for humanity to get to the kingdom, but for the kingdom to get into humanity. The kingdom comes when the reality of heaven penetrates our current reality on earth. This happens when racial barriers collapse, when the sick are healed, when the poor and the rich become friends, when injustices cease, and when hope trumps despair. To pray for God's kingdom to come is to ask for a piece of our future—our perfect future—to insert itself now. And this is more than a prayer we pray with our lips; it is a prayer we live into.

Jesus commissioned the same crowd he taught to pray the Lord's Prayer. In fact, the word he used in Matthew 28:19 was "Go." Most of our churches in the Western world use the marketing phrase "come to us" more than "go into the world." Jesus had in mind a redeemed community whose redemption gave them assignments, tasks, and a mission to live into. Churches aren't social clubs, but outposts. Just as the same God who invites us into baptism also invites us from baptism into meaningful life, the same God who invites us into a weekend worship service also invites us from that worship space into a world he is eager to redeem.

Reclaiming Our Cities

My friend Buddy Bell ministers at the Landmark Church in Montgomery, Alabama. A couple of years ago, he invited me to participate in a sermon series he was doing called Intercession. He specifically wanted me to speak about what it means for the church to intercede for its city and context.

Landmark got creative with the weekend, because they wanted to practice what they preached. They didn't want to teach a form of intercession that they weren't inviting their people into. So they purchased permits for a few locations in downtown Montgomery. A worship service was planned for the steps of the state capitol, and from there, groups would be sent out to pray over a few locations and what they stand for. People were invited, but Landmark had never done this before, so they didn't know what to expect.

When the worship service began, a few hundred people had gathered. We covered the steps of the state capitol. I stood up to speak a few feet from where George Wallace, in 1963, gave his speech: "Segregation yesterday, segregation today, segregation tomorrow." Behind me a few hundred yards was Dexter Avenue Baptist Church, which Dr. King pastored in the late 1950s. I was standing in the middle of historic tension, discussing what it means for people to come together for the sake of the mission of God. Things may be better than they were fifty years ago, but we are far from arriving at a better place. Yet, God's trajectory is toward reconciliation, hope, redemption, and restoration. His heart beats for it. And it is what he invites broken people into.

Embracing Risk and Adventure

At Sycamore View, we like to think that we are a church where broken, hurting people can come and feel accepted, loved, and as if they belong. However, we feel God has helped us progress over the past few years. We don't just want to be a church family where broken people feel like they belong, but we want to exist to faithfully love broken people back to health. In some ways, the church is a hospital, but no one wants to be a permanent resident in a hospital. In fact, hospitals want to heal people so they can be released. If we are not careful, churches can become permanent ICUs, instead of loving people with the expectation that we are preparing them to recover and to live a restored life.

What we have found to be helpful and formative is to help people with brokenness and a past to engage in meaningful ministry and acts of service. It is often when we get out of ourselves that we become more available and willing for Jesus to permeate inside us. It's not that our pain ceases to exist, but that through service we are able to catch a glimpse of how active, alive, and involved our God is throughout the world. Acts of service aren't for those who have it all together. In fact, people in the process of reentry are perfect candidates to be used by God to extend grace, forgiveness, and hope to the world.

At Sycamore View, sometimes this is in the form of connecting people to ministries within our own church. Occasionally, it has been walking the halls of one of our three adopted schools. It may be joining our staff to feed lunch and fellowship with students at HopeWorks, or possibly interacting with former homeless mothers as they transition into permanent housing. Ministry *ministers* to us. It is part of the rhythm that connects us to the heart of God.

It is one of the hardest things to convince people of. Whether it is a parent who has lost a child, a husband who cheated, a person who is drowning in apathy, someone who filed bankruptcy, or a middle-aged man getting serious about an addiction to prescription drugs . . . it is a real challenge to convince people that God hasn't given up on them. I often sit with people who feel like God will still save them, but question if God will ever use them again. God invites us into reentry because there is nothing—nothing— our God cannot redeem and use for his purpose.

So, for all of you who joined me on this journey, to the

> Single mother
> Divorced
> Moral failure
> Depressed
> Grieving
> Addict
> Doubters
> Complacent
> Addicted to politics
> Recovering racists

And to all of us who have been trapped in forms of darkness . . .

Press into God, for he is pressing into you.

Seek the heart of Jesus, for he will not abandon you.

Cling to hope.

Be sustained by his grace.

And for the gracious invitation God continues to give us, extend the same to the world.

PART 5

Resources

Scriptures about Darkness and Light in the Gospels

DARKNESS

Matthew

4:16, 6:23, 8:12, 22:13, 25:30, 27:45

Mark

15:33

Luke

1:79, 11:34, 11:35, 11:36, 22:53, 23:44

John

1:5, 3:19, 8:12, 12:35, 12:46

LIGHT

Matthew

4:16, 5:14, 5:15, 5:16, 6:22, 6:23, 10:27, 24:29

Mark

13:24

Luke

1:79, 2:32, 8:16, 11:33, 11:34, 11:35, 11:36, 12:3, 16:8, 17:24, 23:45

John

1:4, 1:5, 1:7, 1:8, 1:9, 3:19, 3:20, 3:21, 5:35, 8:12, 9:5, 11:9, 11:10, 12:35, 12:36, 12:46

Study Guide

by Luke Norsworthy

Study Guides are tricky, because they take commitment and consistency to do them right. Luke Norsworthy and I discussed at length the best way to go about this. We feel that the best way for you, your team, your small group, or your book club to work through this guide isn't to take a chapter-by-chapter approach, but a section-by-section approach. We want to encourage you to take four to five weeks to work through the main sections of the book together. We feel this will be more helpful, engaging, and efficient.

Thank you, Luke, for your hard work in putting this together. We hope this Study Guide generates healthy conversations.

—*Josh Ross*

Chapter 1

Josh reported that the depression rates and suicide attempts in towns above the Artic Circle are surprisingly not during the fifty-one to sixty-seven days in the winter when the sun doesn't appear. The elevated risks happen when the sun first comes out. Some assume the issue might be the delayed improvement in circumstances, because you see the light before you see the change.

1. Is this a fitting metaphor for life?

You decide that you are going to do the right thing: confess to a friend, go to the meetings, cut off the unhealthy relationship, or see a therapist. Then you expect things to get easier because you've stepped into the light. But just because you've seen the light, doesn't mean that you see the change.

2. Why does the blessing often lag behind the obedience?

Chapter 2

Jesus asks a blind beggar named Bartimaeus in Mark 10:51, "What do you want me to do for you?" Most people could assume what someone in Bartimaeus's situation would want.

1. Why do you think Jesus asks the question?

2. What would your answer be if Jesus asked you what you wanted now?

3. Josh says that new life begins in darkness. How and why?

Part 1: Reentry

Josh describes faith as movement, not just as conversion.

1. How do we experience faith differently when faith is movement, not just a momentary decision?

2. In light of Josh's comfort food issue while in traffic, what are the chances that Josh's arteries are at least 80 percent blocked?

Chapter 3

Josh says many of us don't know how to be free.

1. Why is being free so hard to understand?

Chapter 4

Josh shares, "It has happened too many times to count. I will meet with people in my office, over breakfast, lunch, or coffee, and they will begin to share a hurt, pain, or form of brokenness. And occasionally—the person's age or gender doesn't matter—they will begin to cry.

"Every single time except once, whoever it is that has gotten choked up in front me begins to apologize the moment they begin to weep."

1. Why do we need permission to mourn?

Josh describes how even in a time of Jesus's own suffering, Jesus went to be with the disciples while they were in need.

2. How have you, like the disciples, felt Jesus's presence while you were in a storm of life?

Josh says, "Your identity in Jesus comes before the unhealthy waves of life. The storms don't define us, though they sure will try."

3. How can we let our identity be defined by what God says we are, rather than what we struggle with?

Chapter 5

The school counselor in Barrow said he experiences depression when the sun returns, "because he expects that the light will bring change. However, it doesn't. Instead, as the sun returns, the elements remain. The weather remains the same. The ice won't go away."

1. Have you had a time in your life that you've experienced a breakthrough, yet the surrounding elements stay the same? Did that minimize your breakthrough in your mind?

2. What can we do to still feel the importance of our breakthroughs, even when our surroundings don't seem to reflect the change?

Part 2: Roots

When a tree withstands the winds of a storm, it isn't because of the leaves or branches—which we all see—but rather the roots, which are often hidden from sight, that the tree remains standing.

1. What roots have sustained you during the storms in your life?

Chapter 6

1. Have you ever felt a calling on your life, only to give it up when pain and hardships come your way, arguing that God would clear the path if he really wanted you to do something?

2. How can we keep faith in God's plans for us during times of turmoil?

Chapter 7

Josh confesses, "My heart was not full of anger and bitterness, but I had allowed those things to become lodged in there, and the cancerous effect was slowly spreading."

　1.　How do we let unhealthy thoughts and feelings take root in our heart?

For many of us, we can't live into God's best for us when we still harbor the worst of ourselves in our heart.

　2.　How have you seen changes of heart take place?

Chapter 8

Josh says, "When we acknowledge the vitality of establishing healthy roots, we become proactive, preparing ourselves to remain connected to God through all of the twists and turns in life."

　1.　What would healthy roots look like for you?

Part 3: Rhythms

Josh recounts Henri Nouwen's three phases of the Christian life: solitude, community, and ministry.

　1.　Which comes easiest for you? Which is hardest? Why?

Chapter 9

I've taken these challenges to solitude that Josh mentions and put them in question form. Take ten seconds per question to write the first response that comes to mind. Don't second-guess your answers; just write your initial response down.

Am I more distracted than I am busy?

Am I physically and emotionally exhausted?

How do I handle stress management?

Am I willing to press through growing pains to mature?

Am I spiritually malnourished?

Am I living in denial about my sin and insecurities as well as my need for change?

Do I fear having my heart examined?

1. Are you surprised by your answers?

2. If you could think about the questions longer, would your answers change? If so, why?

Chapter 10

Regarding the story of Josh's affable friend who hurt himself in the weight room:

1. What kind of friend is Josh if he didn't prevent Luke from hurting himself?

2. Is it wrong to not be your brother's/friend's keeper?

(P.S. Only an idiot would hang a seventy-five-pound dumbbell around his neck. I didn't do that. I hung a modest seventy-two-pound weight around my neck.)

Josh describes Rjukan, Norway, which, like Barrow, has a season in which it doesn't receive much or any sunlight. Rjukan added mirrors that would reflect sunlight off surrounding mountains to bring light to the town; and doing so changed the community.

3. Why does having sunlight have such an impact on people?

Like the city of Rjukan, most of us have gone through seasons where we seemed to lack any light.

4. What caused that feeling for you?

5. If you would say that light has been brought back to your soul, what caused that for you?

Chapter 11

Josh describes going into the community to give back (and how he inadvertently bought people beer in Jesus's name). He says, "Some of God's best work through us doesn't come from flowcharts, planned events, or even well-thought-out strategies. It comes from choosing to embrace Jesus's rhythm as our own; and from conviction, kingdom work happens."

1. Can you think of other ways the students could have used that money to positively impact the community?

2. Now that you have some more ideas, what's stopping you from going out and loving on people in Christ's name?

PART 4:
Christmas Trees and Fruit Trees

Josh compares a Christmas tree and a fruit tree. A Christmas tree is for decoration in your house for a few weeks, while a fruit tree stays outside all year round and exists not for self but for those who will enjoy its fruit.

1. In what ways are churches often like Christmas trees?

2. What are the kinds of things a church can do to be more like a fruit tree?

The national director of Celebrate Recovery says we prefer clean over messy, even if the cost for appearing clean is deceit and isolation.

3. How could letting ourselves look a little bit messier help our souls?

4. What does the constant commitment to appear clean do to the soul?

Chapter 12

1. What wells in your life have been partially or wholly filled by Satan at one time or another?

2. What methods did Satan use to put dirt in your well?

3. How can you redig your well so that you can get nourishment again?